Daniel Oshulf
8/22/88

Champion in a Man's World

The Biography of Marion Hollins

David E. Outerbridge

Sleeping Bear Press

Sleeping Bear Press
121 South Main Street
P.O. Box 20
Chelsea, MI 48118

Cataloging-in-Publication Data

Outerbridge, David E.
Champion in a man's world : the biography of
Marion Hollins / David E. Outerbridge
p. cm. ISBN 1-886947-40-6
1. Hollins, Marion, d. 1944. 2. Golfers—United States—
Biography. 3. Women golfers—United States—Biography.
4. Athletes—United States—Biography. 5. Women
athletes—United States—Biography. 6. Golf course
architects—United States—Biography.
I. Title. GV964.H64088 1998
796.352′092—dc21 [B]

98-11410 / CIP

ISBN 1-886947-40-6

Printed and bound in the United States

10 9 8 7 6 5 4 3 2 1

Acknowledgments

I am indebted to many people, without whom this book could never have come into existence.

I owe most special thanks to two individuals. My wife, Lilias Hollins, has tirelessly read the many drafts of the book, and with each reading made essential editorial suggestions. Bob Beck, historian of Pasatiempo, has been a resource for material on Marion's later California years, without which the book would have been meaningless.

I am grateful to the several members of the Hollins family who have supplied important information. Marion's nieces: Phyllis Grissim and Evelina Hoguet; her grandnieces and nephews: Evelina Kats, Judith Lamb, Jean Lawless, Phyllis Theroux, Reginald Frost, and Harry Hollins.

A special thanks to Elizabeth Kuss who has preserved much of the Hollins Long Island history. And to John and Ann Bull and Gail Sanders who preserved Hollins material from Beaufort, South Carolina. Elsewhere on Long Island, my thanks to Thomas Bancroft, Nunzio Ciampi, Elbridge Gerry, Jr., Fred Griffiths, Randolph Harrison, Harry Havemeyer, and James Keresey.

In California, I want to thank Marge Dewey and Saundra Sheffer at the Ralph Miller Golf Library for their support; also William and Nancy Borland, Betty Hicks, Jim Langley, Roger Lapham, and Ray March. And thanks to Pamela Emory for her own research into Marion, and to David White for his research in England. Finally, my appreciation to Maureen Orcutt and the late Virginia Van Wie for sharing their memories of Marion.

Preface

This is a biography of an extraordinary woman who died more than 50 years ago. Her specific, tangible legacy is two golf courses. One, Cypress Point, is often rated either first or second _in the world,_ and is sometimes called the "Sistine Chapel of golf." The Cypress Point Club is private, however, and so, as a legacy, the heirs who may enjoy it are few.

The second course, Pasatiempo, is rated in the country's top 100. Pasatiempo is open to public play, and is, in addition to being a repository into which Marion Hollins poured her life and energy, a lasting tribute to the great golf course architect, Alister MacKenzie.

I would not have undertaken this biography, however, if the legacy was limited to these lasting monuments, extraordinary as they are. What makes Marion Hollins interesting, and important for our—or any—time, is that she was one of those rare human beings who find reward in the achievement itself, with no further external need for confirmation or applause. Said another way, she personified the graceful credo whereby accomplishment is its own reward; that accomplishment is _the_ reward; and the applause, adulation, and attention are superfluous. Although in her day it was an attitude not unusual, Marion's accomplishments were at such an exceptional level that this underlying credo, today largely obsolete, merits recollection.

Today, success is often measured by externals, and we have hoisted "celebrity" to the pinnacle measure of success. The camera focuses only on those who have achieved star status, and though star status may be earned, it may also be purchased with self-serving promotions.

What has happened to the great amateur? It would take a specialist to name more than five in the history of golf, and who can name the top current ones? Where is the coverage of the Walker Cup international matches, let alone their female counterpart, the Curtis Cup?

Marion Hollins, 1892–1944, was a great amateur.* She pursued her interests with an energy some found exhausting. She was stopped by nothing, neither convention nor tradition. And she triumphed. And that was enough. There was too little time to waste it on basking long in the moment; there were other plans to work on.

Marion did not challenge a man's world. Why would she spend time on such a silly pursuit? It reminds me of a bumper sticker seen on Patty Sheehan's car: "Women who seek equality with men lack ambition." But Marion was a *champion* in a man's world because she accomplished things that no woman had, and triumphed in activities which were considered a male province and daunting even to them.

The great boxing trainer, Cus D'Amato, had a saying which he repeated time and time again: "You can if you will, you can't if you won't." It is a little cryptic, but in his life he accomplished what was meant to be not possible. Marion did likewise.

Marion Hollins died in 1944. Fourteen years after her death I married Lilias Hollins, her grandniece. Years passed, until in 1992 I became fascinated with the game of golf. Many were the lost opportunities to talk to aging relatives and friends about Marion. Other missed opportunities stem from my own background. For many years I lived in Rhode Island, down the road from Marion's great friend Glenna Collett Vare, six-time national champion.

The fine Canadian amateur, Sybil Kennedy, with whom Marion competed, was my mother's bridesmaid and best friend. During the weekends she spent with us, she would talk about golf, recalling Marion, but, as no one in the family played the game at that time, whatever she said is forgotten. And since I

---

* I use "amateur" in its true sense, from the French, "to love." An amateur cultivates proficiency in an activity for the love of it, not for the money. In the sporting world earlier in the century, the press and fans reported upon and followed the amateurs more than their professional counterparts. "Amateur" has no connection with its sometimes current use connoting "unprofessional."

began this book, eight other sources I located died before I reached their doorstep.

Moreover, I have not considered it essential to research, for example, every golf tournament that Marion entered, let alone won. She qualified 15 times for the United States Women's Amateur Championship, was runner-up in her first attempt, and in 1921 won the Championship. Among other tournaments, Marion won the venerable Metropolitan Golf Association Championship three times, the Long Island Championship twice, and the Griswald Cup in 1920. She captured the Pebble Beach Championship a record number of eight times, and her course record for women on those links remained unbroken for an extraordinary 16 years.

I have also had to work through errors in reference works. One book, for example, claims that Glenna Collett was captain of the first Curtis Cup team in 1932, when in fact it was Marion's strategic captaincy of the team which brought victory to the United States.

In Marion Hollins's day, people kept scrapbooks, and it is known that she had several. All except one, however, have disappeared, as have almost all of her possessions. Her family's scrapbooks, I was told, had been thrown away when the Hollinses left Long Island. However, in what I consider the reward of persistent research with a dose of the miraculous thrown in, I discovered them, saved from the dump by a woman interested in the social history of the day.*

Tracking down any current knowledge of Marion's equestrian accomplishments proved the most difficult. Prior to World War II, Long Island was the epicenter of polo in the United States—more than 40,000 people came to its North Shore to watch the international matches. No one I interviewed in Long Island, however, had even heard of women playing polo. Yet the newspapers of the day document that Marion was playing polo at Long Island's North Shore and elsewhere with the world's top-ranked male players, both American and British.

---

* There are a number of unattributed quotations in this book from newspapers of the day. Some of them came from clippings which were pasted into these scrapbooks, but without date and identification. From the typeface, I believe they are usually the *New York Times* and the *New York Herald*.

Marion never married and there are no direct descendants who might have preserved at least part of the oral history. Some have found the fact that she never wed curious. As a young woman she was very attractive, almost coquettish in one photograph, and she had many suitors. Dr. Elliott Cutler from Boston wanted to marry her, and Francis Appleton from Ipswich, and later Long Island's North Shore, even booked passage to England to woo her as she crossed the Atlantic headed for another golf tournament. But she would never be tied down into the domestic relationship.

In later years, a teenage niece who was living with her once asked, "Aunt Marion, why aren't you married?"

"Good heavens," she replied, "what would I do with a husband? I don't have enough hours in the day as it is."

A writer who once contemplated authoring a history of the Hollins family stated that he found that the Hollinses did only two things well: making money and raising fine animals. Had he completed the research, he would have discovered that they also had a fine capacity for dramatic failures. Marion was the stunning exception to this last trait, but it has been others—not family—who have kept her extraordinary story alive, most especially the historians of Pasatiempo.

Marion Hollins is buried in a cemetery in Monterey. It is the correct coast for her final resting place. In her life she never drew attention to herself, and so the fact that her grave is marked with a plain generic stone, probably mail-ordered by the family on the East Coast, would have been just fine with her.

Contents

Chapter One

The Enigma of Marion Hollins

A large, wide-shouldered woman, Marion Hollins was far ahead of her time. She was independent, cared little for the niceties of fashion, and most often could be seem striding about in rumpled tweeds. She wore her hair in a severe bob and often donned a cloche hat at a rakish angle for golf. She wore skirts but preferred them to have pockets into which she could thrust her large hands, and she set off a look that can, at best, be called casual.

Marion's many interests set her apart from other women of her day.

—Rhonda Glenn, *Illustrated History of Women's Golf*

The most curious aspect of the Marion Hollins story is that she did not become many times more celebrated than she was. How has this apparent great of American women escaped her deserved legendary status for so long?

Perhaps her inherent modesty caused Marion to shrink from the limelight.

—Betty Hicks, former National Amateur Champion, and a founding member of the LPGA

If Marion Hollins had lived in the TV age, her name would be a household word.

—Kate Rogerson, LPGA touring professional

*O*pera lovers speak of "coloration," the subtle inflection of tones a great singer brings to the notes. The music is written—set—but the way it is shaped and the expression given to a single note, let alone a crescendo or legato, sets a quality that words cannot really describe. The enigma of Maria Callas cannot be netted. It is part of the magic to think about the person and to let the imagination fertilize the picture. Who was the real Anastasia? The mystery of the answer has created a half-century of fascination.

Marion Hollins, born in 1892, will also remain somewhat enigmatic in spite of this biography of words and photographs which give just a partial portrait.

Marion's niece, in her nineties, blind and bedridden, but with the same deep cultured voice, recalls part of the magic of Marion. "She had the most wonderful happy life.... The house was always filled with her friends.... She did so many things.... There was *nothing* she did not know about a horse.... She had an extraordinary friendship among all kinds of people.... Her mother and Marion admired each other, but didn't get on.... Their tastes were very different.... When Marion was staying with them the telephone would never stop ringing."

Can we learn anything from the recollection? Probably not, because the niece's own life had such a large measure of turbulent unhappiness that when she looks back on the scene, the "wonderful happy life" is what the niece experienced when Marion came home to the family place on Long Island. This elderly niece is responding to Marion's coloration, tinted by her own necessarily narrow perspective. The enigma of Marion will never be resolved.

Marion Hollins personally designed the world's most photographed golf hole, the 16th at Cypress Point. She was responsible for the creation of three world-famous golf courses. Although there were architects of record at these courses, she contributed to the architectural design of each, and is cited at the time as "internationally known for her golf, sportswomanship, and *golf architecture*" (emphasis added).

She was America's best female polo player. She was America's leading four-in-hand whip, skilled at driving a coach and four-in-hand team down city streets. She trained jumpers for steeplechase, a sport she introduced to northern California.

She won the Pebble Beach Golf Championship in 1922, 1923, 1924, 1925, 1926, 1928, 1933, and 1942, a record no one has even come close to challenging. She won the Metropolitan Golf Association trophy in 1913, 1919, and 1924. She was United States Amateur Champion in 1921.

She was reportedly the first woman ever to race an automobile in competition.

To my knowledge she is the first woman to devise and develop a planned resort community, built around an overall sporting complex, with established standards for architectural integrity.

She broke hermetic boundaries to mix together old-money society with the great sporting and entertainment figures of the day. Her friends were as diverse as Mary Pickford, Bobby Jones, Spencer Tracy, Harry Payne Whitney, Babe Didrickson, Alfred Gwynne Vanderbilt, Walt Disney, Amelia Earhart, Charlie Chaplin, Will Rogers, and a raft of other personalities.

She was considered the greatest all-around woman athlete of the 1920s, and is arguably the sportswoman of the century.

She encouraged Babe Didrickson and other champions-to-be with their nascent golf game.

She was Athletic Director of Pebble Beach in its formative years. She was the best salesperson in real estate S.F.B. Morse ever had in his development of the Monterey Peninsula and Carmel Valley.

She made a fortune in oil, speculating against expert opinion in the Kettleman Hills.

She was a Suffragette.

She is the tousled, determined looking ten-year-old in a sailor suit. She is the seductive 19-year-old looking out at the

Marion Hollins as a young girl.

camera with a glass of champagne in her hand from her bed aboard the *Lusitania.* She is the woman with the appearance of "a collapsed awning" winning an exhibition match shortly before her death. She is the rider on a bay gelding looking down on land above Santa Cruz that she will buy, with grand plans in mind. She is the woman who packs into Big Sur, consolidates a group of homesteading properties into a purchase of 20 square miles of that coast, with plans to develop a rural retreat. She is a prankster and a gambler, with a highly developed sense of humor.

She was all of these people.

Marion Hollins aboard the Lusitania *in 1910.*
She is a coquettish 18.

Chapter Two

The Beginnings

Family Background

As is commonly known, people develop in part, and in some cases predominantly, in response to the environment into which they are born. The immediate family, the social community, and the physical landscape—not just the natural one, but also the bricks and mortar, frame and timber—all inform the developing consciousness. And habits of the elders, without any conscious effort to be imitated, are usually adopted and incorporated by the next generation. Interests, too.

Marion Hollins was born on December 3, 1892 into a comfortable world, a sporting world, and what was predominantly a man's world.

The Hollins family emigrated from Cheshire, England in 1797, to Baltimore, Maryland, where they became very successful merchants. The family home was "Chatworth," a stately manor which sat on almost 1,000 acres outside the city.

Marion's grandfather, Francis Hollins, married Elizabeth Coles Morris of a wealthy New York family. Her forebears had settled in Massachusetts in 1630 but had moved to Long Island decades before the Revolution, where John B. Coles, Marion's great-grandfather, married Elizabeth Underhill of Oyster Bay. They lived on a large tract of land in Dosoris (now Glen Cove), and are buried at Trinity Church on Wall Street.

Not being tied down by a job, Francis and his wife lived variously in Baltimore, New York, and Paris. In 1854 they bought and settled into a house at 117 Waverly Place in Manhattan.

Marion's father, Harry Hollins, and two sisters and a brother grew up in New York City with their mother, who divorced her husband on adultery charges. She was a well educated woman, and even wrote a book, *The History of Civilization,* for Marion's brother. Either her knowledge petered out in the classical period, or she became bored, because the history ends at the year 65 B.C.

Determined that her son Harry would get his education at Harvard, in due course she sent him off to Cambridge, where he joined his fun-loving pal, Amedee de Pau Moran.

"We certainly had a grand time," he reflected, "but after a week came to the conclusion we could drink as much in New York and play as much poker."

So Harry Hollins returned to New York and began work as a runner on Wall Street. He was soon hired at $400/annum by Morton Bliss & Co., where he learned much about foreign exchange. From there he moved to another firm where he dealt with orders on the Curb. At just eighteen, he moved yet again to a position of cashier/bookkeeper.

Shortly thereafter, during the panic of 1873, Harry Hollins had his first chance to prove himself a significant player in the business of the day. The market was in a severe decline, and his firm had entered into financial contracts (puts) which exposed them to severe losses in a down market, as well as obligations they could not honor. Mr. Cummings of Cummings & Co. tried to climb over the partition into the cashier's section to force his stocks on them, but Harry disposed of him and then closed the firm early so creditors could not get in. The next day, as the market continued to weaken and the company had no way to meet its obligation, Harry hid the partner in the back room. As messengers arrived for payment he sent them back for more explicit instructions, thus stalling the run until 3 P.M. when the Exchange closed. This panic was severe enough to keep the Exchange closed for a month.

In 1877 Harry Hollins married Evelina Meserole Knapp, and started his own company. Two years later, he bought his own seat on the Exchange. For the first few years of their marriage they lived at different addresses in New York City, but soon had their own house as well as a country place in East Islip, Long Island.

Harry, Marion's father, was very much a "club man," not untypical of a successful businessman of the day from the correct social background. He belonged to the Union, Metropoli-

Marion's father, Harry Bowly Hollins,
with her brother Jack.

tan, South Side Sportsman, Knickerbocker, Westminster Kennel, Downtown, Lawyer's, New York Yacht, Racquet, Meadow Brook, and St. Andrews clubs. He later joined the Garden City Golf Club and the Links, among others.

Marion's mother, Evelina Meserole Knapp Hollins, traced her lineage back to the Plymouth Colony. She was a highly cultured woman with a strong personality. A family friend and contemporary of Marion, Schuyler Parsons, who spent his life floating through society observing its niceties, wrote: "The lack of taste in my father's generation was extraordinary, but fortunately not universal.... Evie Hollins [was] exempt from the common blight...among the first to get away from the brownstone, high stoop, narrow house, and build on a two-lot frontage what were known as English Basement houses, Georgian in design and filled with beautiful French and English things of the eighteenth century instead of Victorian horrors.... Her exquisite taste was able to make a farmhouse on Long Island or an old cottage in Beaufort, South Carolina, a fitting frame for her beautiful character." Edith Wharton had also cast her condemnation of brownstone: "universal chocolate coating of the most hideous stone ever quarried."

The family's winter home was a house commissioned of pink brick at 12-14 West 56th Street. It was five stories high and was one of the largest residences south of Central Park. This was a very fashionable location. Neighbors included Iselins, Satterlees, Forbeses, and Laphams. The property included two lots on the street with much more land behind, which was later sold for a hotel site. (Today the building at 12-14 West 56th Street houses the Embassy of Argentina.)

The Vanderbilt Connection

In 1880, Harry Hollins became a confidant of William K. Vanderbilt, and before long the two families were virtually inseparable. The men did business together, and the families shared common interests in Long Island where they had magnificent estates nearby.

In 1884, William K. Vanderbilt's father went abroad, and during his absence a panic hit. Harry Hollins and his wife and the Vanderbilts moved into the 5th Avenue Hotel, as they dared not leave the city during the crisis. Hollins & Co. was the clearinghouse for other Vanderbilt brokers as well as doing a large business with the family in its own right.

Harry knew the market was going to be weak and that they would need more securities as collateral to weather the day. He informed Vanderbilt of this during breakfast. The latter replied that there were none at hand, but that he had cabled his father to instruct the bank to open the vault, but no word had come back.

Marion Hollins's mother, Evelina Meserole Knapp Hollins.

Harry Hollins recalled, "I was eating buckwheat cakes at the time and one stopped right in my throat. For months after, I didn't care much about buckwheat cakes."

He went to his partner and they agreed that as the Vanderbilts had always done everything for them, it was time now to come to their aid. They produced their entire package of unpledged securities to back the falling prices on Vanderbilt railroad stocks. It came to only $400,000 but was enough to carry the accounts until the cable arrived authorizing the Union Trust Company to open the Vanderbilt vault.

"That such a relatively small amount should have served to stem a panic selling is interesting," reflected Harry Hollins, but the fact that he had pledged everything in the moment of crisis bonded forever the Vanderbilt–Hollins friendship, a friendship which continued through Marion's generation.

"Meadowfarm"

Meadowfarm was a 600-acre parcel of land in East Islip, running to the Great South Bay and bordered on one side by Champlin's Creek. Formerly the Mainwaring Farm, Harry Hollins bought it in 1880, and built a large house set in the midst of sweeping lawns and meadows with a view out across the bay to Fire Island. The three-story structure was painted a dark red and was distinguished by a great number of gables. Breezy porches faced in three directions.

At the time Marion Hollins was born, Meadowfarm was a scene from a film: the sun is rising on the grand house set in its extensive lawns. The cocks are crowing, and the farm and stable hands and gardeners are leaving their quarters for the daily chores. Meadowfarm is almost a self-contained community, akin to the great manors in Europe. There is the icehouse, piggery, gardens, greenhouses, barns, stables, and many outbuildings. There are coachmen, cowmen, gardeners, grooms, and the entire indoor staff, including Mrs. Hollins's personal maid and Mr. Hollins's valet. Thanks to the kindness of Mrs. Hollins, Meadowfarm is also home to an indigent old soldier, veteran of Longstreet's troops at Gettysburg, who lives in one of the outbuildings and obtains food from the main house's kitchen.

*The main house at Meadowfarm, Marion Hollins
in baby carriage.*

Stables at Meadowfarm.

*Cow barn with its clock tower at Meadowfarm,
designed by Richard Morris Hunt.*

*The remodeled farmhouse the family moved into after
Harry Hollins went bankrupt and was forced
to sell the big house.*

The barns, stables, and carriage house were immense, the former mounted with a graceful clock tower. (As an idea of scale, the carriage house was remodeled in this century into a 19-room residence.)

Also on the Meadowfarm grounds was a classic eighteenth century farmhouse, once the property of Walt Whitman's uncle. Later, just before World War I when bankruptcy forced Harry Hollins and his family to move out of the big house at Meadowfarm, they settled into what they called "the farmhouse."

Until then, this building had been the caretaker's cottage. Marion's nieces laugh when they recall the name. "The so-called farmhouse had three living rooms, a billiards room, and a three-hole golf course."

The family dock secured boats for rowing, sailing, and gunning. Champlin's Creek provided good fishing, while the marshes were rich in aquatic game birds, perfect for the menfolk who loved their fowling.

East Islip, although perhaps never as posh as Long Island's North Shore enclaves, nonetheless was a very fashionable community, peopled by some of old New York's wealthy families who preferred the South Shore where the prevailing summer southwest breeze swept in across the ocean and bay, cooling the great houses.

Marion's Early Days

The Hollins family, from late spring until the fall, if they were not traveling in Europe, stayed at Meadowfarm, and it is there we must look at the early years of Marion Hollins to find the fiber of her life and interests.

From the time she could walk and first began to talk, Marion was on the move. The Long Island Hollins estate, Meadowfarm, invited it. Active parents and four brothers ensured it.

Sports were a part of life, "the purpose of life," according to one family member. They were a social activity which was included in the day's routine, even on a Sunday after church. Horses were central, much as the combustion engine is for us today. Although it was the twilight of horse transport, the *horseless* carriage was still just a plaything of the wealthy.

Marion Hollins as a young girl.

Marion Hollins on steamer en route to Europe with her parents and older brother.

As a primer for all her future accomplishments, Marion Hollins had been born in the right place and time. The difference between her and other women who were starting from a similar vantage was, perhaps, that from the beginning she felt bound by no convention when it limited life's possibilities.

It takes a strong personality to run against accepted practice, especially in those years of the Gilded Age when within the family matrix it was a time of governesses and tutors, when children were to be seen and not heard, and expected to be summarily obedient.

Parents often smile at, and tolerate, daughters who are tomboys, however. Mothers, perhaps because they inwardly applaud the rebellion against conformity. Fathers, well, because the girl is showing the man's own prowess—her father's little girl.

At the age of three, what was Marion thinking about? One thing which was to dominate her interest for the rest of her life was horses.

Marion Hollins on her mother's lap, learning to drive.

She was at the reins of a runabout at age four, and was in the saddle of a pony before that. She was in the stable, and in the tack room. She learned from horses and about them until there was no more to learn. All the family were comfortable driving or in the saddle; could jump, hunt, exhibit. This in itself was not exceptional, but Marion achieved a pinnacle of expertise way beyond her siblings, parents, nieces, and nephews. "There was *nothing* she did not know about a horse," her ninety-year-old niece reiterated.

Because it was part of family life, and her father's and brothers' interest, she also learned golf and tennis. We don't know if she also shared their love of bird hunting and boating, although there are photos of her at about age nine displaying a row of ducks. Undoubtedly she went with them out to Hollins Island for picnics, and on to Fire Island, for ocean swimming. Hollins Island (also known as Greater Fire Island) had been bought by the Nicoll family in 1687 from Winnequeheagh, sachem of Connetquot. In 1906 Harry Hollins purchased it from the estate of Sarah Nicoll and subsequently gave it to his sons.

*Marion Hollins, age 12, winning the blue ribbon in the
saddle class at the Bayshore Horse Show.*

Approximately 50 acres in size, Hollins Island was situated
in the Great South Bay near the Fire Island inlet. At one time
cut for its salt hay, it was converted to a hunting preserve for
the family. They built a cottage, docks, and a few outbuildings
for comfort in their outings.

All types of waterfowl frequented its marshes, ponds, and
shoreline, and, just to make certain that there were ample ducks,
the caretaker used to corn the ponds, "ready prey to the accu-
rate marksmanship of the Hollins family."

In 1919, a member of the family shot a barnacle goose, so
rare that only five specimens had ever been identified in the
United States. It is now in the Natural History Museum in New
York.

Today the island is a nature preserve.

Marion grew up in an idyllic world of open lands, friends,
animals, and the games children enjoy. She and her brothers

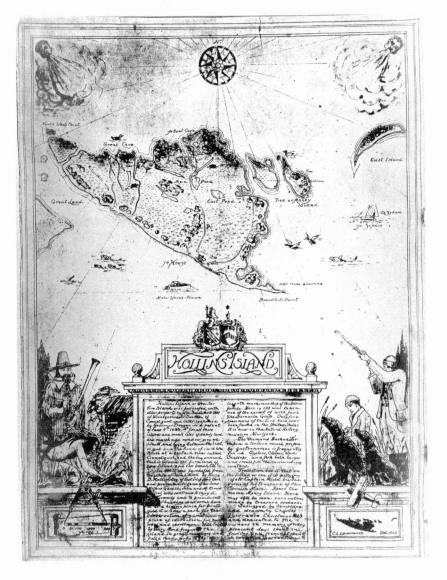

accompanied their parents on their grand trips to attractive places where they were invited to stay and play with the paragons of society. However, there was a less pretty side which made all of this possible.

Harry Hollins' Business

The financial empires which were made and lost, including that of Harry Hollins, were built on a free-form conduct which exceeded what even a reasonable standard of laissez-faire might suggest.

These were the robber barons. They manipulated companies and stocks to rob from each other as well as from the public. "The public be damned" is still remembered today as the much-publicized expostulation of Commodore Vanderbilt. "Law? What do I care for law? Hain't I got the power?" was another of his pronouncements.

Many of these battles took place over control of the nation's growing infrastructure: the railroads, tunnels, bridges, and utilities. It was in this maelstrom of skulduggery that Harry Hollins made his name and fortune, and ultimately went bankrupt.

It was a tiny world in which everyone knew everyone, and business was done in the drawing rooms of private mansions or men's clubs. It was an age when club affiliation carried every importance—an entree to the people making the deals, the contacts to pursue business goals without having to go to the street for backing.

It must be remembered that this was not the Mafia in operation. These gentlemen were the social leaders of the day. It also was a time when, one columnist reported, "Most of the Biddles and Cadwaladers [prominent Philadelphia families] now are either in front of bars or behind bars." (Quoted in Louis Auchincloss's *The Vanderbilt Era*.)

And Marion's brother told her nephew, "Not all the members of the [Harvard's elite] Porcellian Club have been to prison. But everyone I have ever known who has been to prison was a member of the Porcellian Club."

In 1913, H.B. Hollins & Co. failed.* The gates to the most prestigious space in the financial district, the entire ground floor of the building which cuts a corner out of the New York

---

* In his day, Harry Hollins financed and controlled: Banco Hipotecario de Mexico, the International Mortgage Bank of Mexico, all the gaslight companies in St. Louis, the 23rd Street Ferry Company, Union Ferry Company, Hoboken Ferry Company, and Brooklyn Ferry Com-

Stock Exchange, at Broad and Wall Streets, were closed and locked. Harry Hollins, wife and family moved to the farmhouse. Mrs. Hollins auctioned her large collection of tapestries, furniture, rare books, and paintings including works by George Romney and Sir Joshua Reynolds.

Charles Lawrance and his wife bought the main house at Meadowfarm and moved in. Lawrance was the creator of the Whirlwind Engine which powered the planes of both Lindbergh and Amelia Earhart, visitors both to Meadowfarm.

The Gilded Age

Marion Hollins was growing up at the epicenter of what Mark Twain labeled "The Gilded Age," and what John Kenneth Galbraith later described as "a world of competitive ostentation."

The Gilded Age was a time of extravagance and at the same time an age manqué. Ornate mansions, some used for only a few weeks a year, were constructed of marble, wainscoting, friezes, and mantels torn from the estates of impoverished European nobles. Some estates employed over 100 servants for the house and grounds. If a mansion contained 70 rooms, over 30 typically were for servants. In one exchange, a college student telegraphed his mother from Harvard, "Arriving with a crowd of 96 men." To which she replied, "Many guests already here. Have only room for 50."

It was a time of high-stake shooting sprees, when scores of birds might be shot in a single morning by a couple of contestants. There were yachts with crews in the dozens always at the ready. Costume balls which cost hundreds of thousands of dollars were frequent entertainment. Like the fool's scepter, these were the baubles of success, and fools with nothing better to do such as Ward McCallister, self-appointed arbiter of who was acceptable in social circles, created lists for ranking these mem-

---

pany. His company also financed the organization of the United States Rubber Company, the Brooklyn Rapid Transit Corporation, and the East River Gas Company (which supplied Manhattan), among others.

bers of society, with the result that families went to ever-greater excess to ensure inclusion on the lists.

It was a day when these families considered the East Coast the only acceptable place to live, the West being almost aboriginal. "Yachts have of late come into the wrong hands. People from Detroit or somewhere." But as the new century moved ahead, the old walls of the social redoubt would crack and crumble. Edith Wetmore in her Chateau Sur Mer in Newport, Rhode Island noted the change: "We're the end of an era, if you please," she remarked when she looked out and could count only eight families of "proper lineage."

It was a time of posture, and the puffery of prescribed etiquette. Relationships and a lifetime could go by without the grist of real emotions, or even impassioned conversation. It was a time when you didn't even "look out loud." A member of the set, and a friend of Marion's, would write looking back on the period: "The burning question for a man was whether to wear a white or black tie for the evening."

Mimicry of English upper class life was everywhere: riding to hounds, the various racquet games, polo, golf, and cricket, all were direct imports. Servants were dressed in livery, and for grand events even wore powdered wigs. Lavender water, lace doilies, and other notions were imported from London's chic Jerymn Street. Private schools and tutors taught the children of society English spellings; e.g., harbour, colour, theatre; and the letter "z" was pronounced "zed."

What was it that compelled these leaders of society to mimicry? Because it was so splendid it begged to be copied? Or because it provided some sort of authentication that one had "arrived"?

These families, scions of a self-described gentry, stayed among themselves. "[They are] cold to the point of rudeness when they don't know you, but if they do, the most dependable friends," commented Schuyler Parsons. Like the proverbial birds of a feather, they moved to their seasonal watering places *en masse*. And migrate they did, for "the season." There was a winter "season" of several weeks in the Carolinas, when New York became too raw. There were country places for "the season" in spring and autumn; and to Europe for "the season" several weeks in summer. Then, of course, there was Saratoga for the "racing season," and Newport for the "summer season" of balls.

One little party typifies the somewhat wanton behavior of the day. The Hollinses were having a fancy dress ball at Meadowfarm. The night was getting on, spirits were high, as the spirits were flowing. In the smoking room—a male preserve—came the impromptu suggestion: meet in the morning at the Islip train station, bring a set of golf clubs, and see what happens. A few prior arrangements had been made by one of the partyers, including a private railcar to be attached to the New York bound 7:49.

Private railroad cars were, if not exactly the norm of the period, owned by many of the financially successful titans of the day, and this one had been produced by Percy Pyne II whose family were large landowners on the South Shore. The happy revelers, in addition to Pyne, included Marion's brothers, Jack and McKim Hollins.

After arriving in New York City, the car was switched to a train heading for Tuxedo Park. There they were greeted by Pierre Lorillard of the tobacco fortune. Lorillard had formerly lived close to the Hollins place, but had moved north of New York City and founded a private community. After being entertained at lunch, there was golf on the Tuxedo course. That evening a dinner party was given in the newcomers' honor, with a band. The party car was then attached to a series of trains which brought it eventually to Philadelphia, having recruited more revelers. More golf, more dinners. This moveable happiness then continued along the rails for almost a week, adding and losing conscripts, until the car finally pulled into Grand Central Station, for a final farewell dinner at Delmonicos.

And what of these gentlemen who called themselves sportsmen? They felt nothing amiss in killing hundreds of migratory birds and, at a time before regulation, at any time of year. And woe to any animal, furry or feathered, that entertained predatory ideas about the South Side Sportsmen's Club's fish or game. Gamekeepers were hired to destroy the undesirables. In the last decade of the nineteenth century this included the killing of:

36	fox
42	raccoon
644	opossum
39	skunk
104	mink

59	weasel
46	woodchuck
1031	muskrat
286	osprey
332	hawk
54	owl
108	Great blue heron
25	night heron (quawk)
70	green heron
262	kingfisher
411	jay
208	crow
29	rattle snake
279	black snake
26	puff adder

Furthermore, these animals were not killed just because they were chanced upon. They were *lured*. Nothing was thought of the use of decoys to bring in the trout-eating great blue herons so that they could be shot.

Marion's father wrote with admiration of the marksmanship of one South Side member. "I have seen him shoot hummingbirds from the club piazza on trees twenty and thirty yards away, and I never saw him miss." Perhaps he ran out of birds, because in his later years this sport amused other members by shooting the ashes off their cigars while in their mouths.

These were the families of enormous wealth; sometimes inherited, sometimes made in the rough and tumble frontier atmosphere of unregulated monopoly building. The Gilded Age was a period of a few decades when the gilt was everywhere and the guilt nowhere to be found.

The Hollins family was part of it all.

There were many casualties within the privileged families of the Gilded Age, but there were also many survivors. Marion not only survived, she triumphed.

The early years of Marion and her four brothers were idyllic. Imagine life at Meadowfarm from her perspective.

Surrounding the main house were lawns, meadows, orchards, and gardens. Hammocks swung under tree limbs, and outdoor furniture was laid out in shady spots. A tennis court was set up on a leveled, closely mown section of the lawn. A

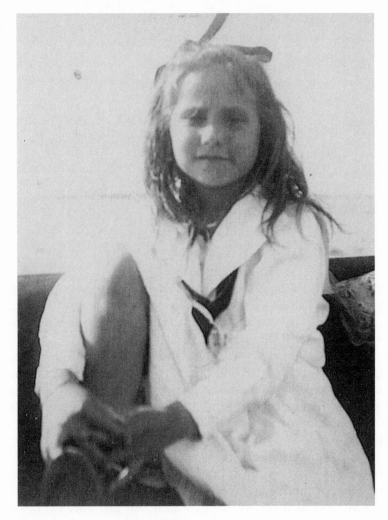

Marion, tomboy at ten.

three-hole golf course was laid out in another area. Then there were the stables. Like her forebears, horses became part of Marion's knowledge almost from the age of walking. Riding and driving were as natural then as hopping into an automobile today, but without the age restrictions. The Hollins carriage house contained the typical assortment of rigs for that day: landaus, runabouts, gigs, barouches, broughams, and coaches.

The stables, accordingly, housed a variety of horses bred for specific purposes. Marion could always be found here, currycombing the horses, saddle-soaping the tack and scouring the bits, before putting her pony through its paces with a gallop bareback around the property.

Marion's mother, a breeder of collies, loved animals, a trait she passed on to her daughter. Mrs. Hollins would coax birds to the outdoor tea table with crumbs, and could imitate their songs. She had a large pet snake which lived on the porch where there was always a bowl of milk for it. And she was especially fond of the pony she had given Marion, named Daisy. She used to amuse her young daughter and her playfriends by calling for Daisy, which, to the despair of the gardener, would trample through the flower beds and trot up onto the porch and nuzzle Mrs. Hollins to find the lump of sugar in her pocket.

Later, Marion adopted her mother's playful relationship with the pony. She used to amuse her nieces by playing hide and seek with the animal, and once took it into the house upstairs to visit someone in bed. This latter anecdote is often mentioned in the family, and I imagined the young girl leading her pony up the staircase. This image is correct up to a point. Marion had brought the pony into the house, down the hall, and up the staircase and into her sister-in-law's bedroom where the recumbent lady was enjoying breakfast in bed. But the year was 1924. Marion was not a young girl, she was *thirty!* I exclaimed at this to her niece, an eyewitness. "Of course. Marion would have done it at 50."

Even at a young age Marion was possessed of a fierce independence and sense of what was fair. Once she and her mother got into a tiff, until, with voices rising, her mother said: "We will end this discussion *right now.* Go upstairs and prepare yourself for dinner." Marion turned on her heel and went to her room. There she took a pair of scissors and proceeded to cut off clumps of her hair until her head was shorn. Then she strode downstairs into the parlor and announced to her mother, "I am now prepared for dinner."

Marion's twin brothers were five years older. A pair of toughs, they were often caught making trouble. Their mother's punishment was to make them play with Marion and her friends, which of course they hated. They taught the girls cruel tricks like making slingshots and shooting at cats. They also taught them "boy" things such as how to pick up crabs and snapping turtles from the creek without getting bitten.

Though extravagantly opulent, the Gilded Age also had a genuine genteel quality to it. Mrs. Hollins, as was typical of the day, carefully pasted photographs into scrapbooks, while guestbooks were filled with toasts, drawings, poesy and other appreciations. One can almost glean a social history from these volumes. The grandson of the author of the *Night Before Christmas* penned the entire poem in one of the leather bound books. Francis Appleton and Devereux Milburn, great polo players from the North Shore of Long Island, are frequent signers in the guestbooks, complementing their signatures with sketches of horses clearing hedges. Seating arrangements for dinner parties were carefully drawn in the books.

It was a time when gentlemen tipped their hats to each other and lifted them for ladies. And then there were the calling cards requiring a special etiquette: turning up the left upper corner meant the caller had stopped by; turning the upper right corner was a visit to congratulate on a wedding or other happy event. A flat card meant something else. There were yet other conventions in the case when a wife or manservant delivered the card. And of course there was a silver tray in the hall to receive these cards. It was a time of strict etiquette, including a prescribed formula for flirtation.

In the early years of the new century, Harry Hollins was doing business internationally and traveling with his family to Europe more frequently than business required. As he was friendly with many of England's titled society including the Prince of Wales (later Edward VII), Consuelo Vanderbilt (then Duchess of Marlborough) and many others, they were frequent guests in the country manors, spent race week at Cowes aboard J.P. Morgan's *Corsair,* and played golf at Sandwich and other notable courses. There are snapshots of Marion at about age six with her father on the golf course at Royal St. George's. On another trip she accompanied her father and Morgan to their audience with the Pope.

For the Hollins family, the Atlantic crossing was virtually an annual event. In those days the *Social Register* used to include, in addition to the normal address and club affiliations, sailing notices. The Hollins family entry for 1910, for example, notes, "departing July 28, *Lusitania,* returning September 24."

Marion's mother used these trips to Europe for extensive shopping for clothes and linens, an interest somehow never passed on to her daughter. In fact, Marion became almost famous for her disregard of appearance, and was usually dressed in a rumple of baggy sweaters and skirts. And, in disregard of etiquette, when visiting the grand families she would often leave the main part of the house and spend the evening playing poker with the male servants.

In Paris, Marion was given driving lessons by the legendary whip, Edwin Howlett. At the age of nine she drove a coach-and-four up the Champs Elysees.

Driving a team of four requires considerable skill, and needs strong arms and endurance as well. Like the golf swing, there are subtleties in the execution. "Never let your horses know you are driving them, or, like women, they may get restive. Do not pull and haul and stick your arms akimbo, but keep your hands as though you were playing the piano." This advice from one expert of the time (male, obviously). Marion had a voracious appetite for practice. At home she harnessed four-in-hand reins to four weights and pulled them in the various maneuvers *hundreds of times* every day. She also spent hours working on the whip.

Although the press coverage of her as a famous whip of her day was confined to this country, there is nonetheless a marvelous photo of her taken at age 18, sitting on the box, turning a team into a side street in Paris. The newspaper caption reads, "Driving her four-in-hand through the narrowest streets in Paris."

Thus by the time she was 20, Marion was very familiar with Britain and France, and would soon be journeying abroad on her own, a welcome guest of the large number of friends she had made.

And so it was in a life of privilege she grew up, with years that were carefree in the truest sense of the word. She practiced and played sports; she went abroad in comfortable circumstances; was invited to Aiken, South Carolina and Palm Beach "for the season" with her parents, and later to hunt, play polo, and golf on her own.

Her four brothers, perhaps because in the eyes of their parents they could do no wrong, were rowdies. They smashed furniture and windows at Brown's Hotel in London. They ran around

Meadowfarm naked no matter the company. Jack threw his twin brother over a wall, breaking his leg, causing Gerald to limp for the rest of his life. Even after they became adults, with one exception they were best known as charming alcoholics. Marion, however, remained unspoiled by her life of privilege.

As Marion grew into womanhood, she displayed a well-developed sense of civic responsibility. When the United States edged toward World War I she took all her trophies, 38 of them, to be melted down for the war effort. Included were the runner-up trophy for the United States Women's Amateur Golf Championship, and the winner's cup for the Metropolitan Golf Association tournament. She donned a Red Cross uniform and made bandages for the front. And when a large merchant ship foundered off Long Island in a storm and the crew struggled ashore through the surf after abandoning ship, she was there in a slicker and sou'wester serving hot drinks on the beach to the survivors.

She marched under the Suffragette banner "Failure is Impossible." It was so much her own credo one wonders if she coined the slogan. She was photographed by the press on the avenues and at City Hall rallying support for women's right to vote.

Her most noted patriotic feat, featured even a quarter-century later in her obituary, was driving a coach-and-four from Buffalo to New York City and down 5th Avenue to raise money for Liberty Bonds. In the spring of 1918, Marion Hollins hitched up Alfred Vanderbilt's aging greys to the famous coach "Liberty" and embarked on one of the great drives of history. Along the more than 450-mile trek she stopped to raise money for the war effort at scores of towns and villages as she headed east to Albany, and then south for the final run to Manhattan.

THE VANDERBILT GREYS

The renowned old team in harness again, helping to avenge their master, who went to his death on the Lusitania, by their service to the country in the third Liberty Loan. Although their aggregate age was 84 years, these noble horses made the trip and arrived at City Hall, New York, in such good condition that the late Judge Moore said, "They look as well as I ever saw them and fit for the show ring today." Photo taken at the Half Way sign post which was erected at the suggestion of Frank D. Lyons, then road commissioner. Miss Marian Hollins, (golf, tennis, in fact all round sportswoman) driving, Morris E. Howlett beside her, Mr. F. D. Lyons standing at the sign-board.

Chapter Three

Getting Ready

She spent hours every morning perfecting this or that shot, sometimes with the professional to give her advice, but more often alone with a caddie to chase her balls.

—Dorothy Noyes, at Pebble Beach

One reason Marion's trophies have disappeared is because she had no use for them. If someone admired a particular silver cup or plate, she'd just give it away.

—Phyllis Grissim, her niece

*M*arion possessed two traits which today are rarely combined. She worked tremendously hard and with great diligence to perfect her sporting skills. At the same time, she retained only fleeting interest in victory. Often she did not attempt to follow up on a victory by defending her title the following year. If the timing was right she would play the tournament, but she could just as easily be off on an entirely different quest.

She competed hard, "like a man," but never engaged in gamesmanship. Younger players against whom she competed described how she would go out of her way to fortify them during a round. Clara Callender, who as a seventeen-year-old defeated Marion in the annual Pebble Beach Championship in 1937, recalls being "very green and naive," and recounts how Marion, jovial and laughing, was constantly a helpful presence.

In another championship, California reporter Ann Trabue commented: "It was a great match to watch, an exhibition of fine sportsmanship, the older player encouraging the younger. 'It was a hard match to lose,' said Miss Hollins as she shook hands with her opponent after winning on the 19th hole, and Helen [Lawson], a little dismayed at losing a match in which she was never down and in which she was three up and four to go, smiled bravely as she chalked up her defeat to inexperience."

In the *Green Book of Golf, 1923–4* (a hardcover annual chronicle of the sport in California), the frontispiece is a photograph of Marion seated on a bench with J.W. Byrne. The caption reads "Lady Practice and Lord Theory."

As a teenager and until late in her life, she was often at the golf course practicing. In the early decades there was no such thing as a practice range. In those days, traffic was usually light

"Golf Royalty"
Marion Hollins and J.W. Byrne,
Lady Practice and Lord Theory.

on the course, and it was normal to practice from the first tee down the fairway. A shag boy, or junior caddie, would then collect the practice balls. Fred Griffiths, son of her first teacher, remembers how Marion would come out late in the afternoon at the nine-hole Westbrook course just down the road from Meadowfarm to practice hitting ball after ball down the course into the evening.

The enormous amount of practice preparing for a tournament would seem to dictate that winning was paramount. Not so for Marion. Although she won hundreds of tournaments, matches, and trophies, she paid little attention to her successes, nor ever made anything of them in conversation. She never had a space devoted to the display of her cups and ribbons. They didn't matter. Life was moving on to the next adventure.

Even in the midst of a competition, conquest was not a consuming interest. Cecil Leitch, the great British champion, observed that Marion "[appears] to be happiest when hitting out from the tee or on the putting green, but who has little interest in the in-between shots." Adrian Wilson, Marion's caddie from the Pasatiempo days, confirms this. He told her niece that Marion's mind would drift off in the middle of a match into visions of the next big thing she was going to do. "I had to keep her inspired," he recalled.

Marion entered every activity fearlessly. This fearlessness, combined with a positive outlook and the feel for her sport, allowed her to drive golf balls across the chasm, and to maintain her credo that failure is impossible. Because of her confidence, she was disarming to competitors one and all. She would give to every effort her massive positive energy, and then smile at its conclusion, whatever it might be.

Chapter Four

The Early Sporting Years

My earliest recollection of the South Side Club is of my mother and grandmother Morris telling me how my great uncle, Archibald Coles, used to drive four-in-hand from Dosoris, now Glen Cove, to Liff Snedecor's Tavern at Islip, taking my grandfather and grandmother Morris with him. It was from her I learned of the parties made up for the deer hunting and how Morris's stand was situated below the upper brook, about 100 yards from the present hatchery, and Mr. Lorenzo Delmonico's (the original Delmonico) farther down. After one of these deer drives Mr. Delmonico was found dead on his stand from a heart attack from deer excitement.

—Harry Hollins in "Happy Hunting Ground, Recollections of the South Side Sportsman's Club," 1936

The Southside Sportsmen

The first sporting attraction of the South Shore of Long Island in the middle of the last century was the fishing and hunting, and the establishment of the South Side Sportsman's Club cemented for eight decades the area as a gathering place for some of New York's oldest families. The South Side Club was a men-only refuge. It was to be near here that Marion's parents, uncles, and cousins, as well as Vanderbilts, Cuttings, Havemayers, Livingstons, Wilmerdings, and others built their country homes. The club even had its own private railroad station so that members could proceed directly from New York City to their refuge. (The South Side Club stands today, but is now a state-run nature study facility. The members are gone, but two relics of their heyday exist: recipes for "Southsides," a gin-based drink which is still served in Long Island; and "clams Southside" which was served at breakfast at the club as a restorative for those who had too many of the former the evening before.)

Even as the South Side Club continued to attract members, other sports were beginning to appear on the horizon.

Golf

In Scotland, golfers had been making paths down the links when it was still an age of bow and arrow, dirks and swords, and when self-righteous people were burning witches at the stake. Mary Queen of Scots was accused by her political enemies of playing golf shortly after the death of her husband, a sign of callousness and poor decorum.

However, it was only four years before Marion was born that the game of golf was introduced into the United States. True, there had been claims of a fleeting attempt at the sport in Savannah in 1795, Charleston in 1786, Chicago in 1875, Burlington, Iowa in 1883, Oakhurst, West Virginia in 1884. It was in 1888, however, that a group of gentlemen who had enjoyed hitting golf balls into some soup cans set into a pasture a short distance north of New York City sat down and, over a few Scotches, created the first 18-hole golf club named, appropriately, St. Andrews. John Reid, who had called the meeting, is often dubbed the father of golf in this country. This credit must be shared, however, with Robert Lockhart who had come to settle in New York City from his birthplace of Dunfermline, Scotland. The previous year Lockhart was in Scotland and bought a set of clubs and two dozen gutta percha balls from Old Tom Morris at St. Andrews. He brought them back. Lockhart took his sons and the new equipment up to a meadow near the Hudson River (where today 72nd street and Riverside Drive intersect) and proceeded to test his clubs, playing up and down the unpopulated riverside. People out walking thought the novel activity looked foolish.

Harry Hollins, familiar with the game from his trips to Britain, soon became a member of the newly formed St. Andrews Club in Yonkers.

In the same year, Horace Hutchinson was invited by a member of the Meadow Brook Hunt on Long Island's North Shore to demonstrate the new game of golf to his fellow sportsmen. Meadow Brook, which two decades later would draw Marion Hollins to the North Shore for its hunt, polo, and horse shows, was centered in equestrian pursuits and not at all ready for golf. Horace Hutchinson, however, was two-time winner of the British championship, and a well-known all-around sportsman, so the club members were happy to oblige him in his demonstration. He arrived dressed in the elegant golfing garb of his homeland. This was not unlike the dress of the hunt: long scarlet coat with velvet trim and brass buttons, knickers (resembling jodhpurs), stockings (which from a distance resemble riding boots), gaiters, and shoes.

Even Hutchinson's demonstration, coupled with the fact that the gentlemen of the Meadow Brook Hunt were interested in sports generally, could not draw an approving nod to the game that he displayed for them. He later wrote: "My exhibition was not very effective as they did not seem to think it meant much. They tried the clubs for themselves and the result was not such as to give them a very exalted opinion of the game. The most favorable criticism that I can recall was that it might be a good game for Sunday afternoons. I do not think it was extravagant praise."

Within a few years, golf became a part of the club activity, but foxhunting retained its popularity. Then, some years later, came a more serious menace to the foxhunting population. This was Robert Moses with his ideas for a network of parkways on Long Island. He was presented to the members of Meadow Brook. "To the fox hunters in their red coats," he recalled, "[we] explained the Northern Parkway. Whereupon the audience rose as one man, and denounced us on the grounds the hounds would lose the scent as the foxes crossed the parkway."

In 1889, W.K. Vanderbilt happened to be in Biarritz with some friends where they encountered a young Scot, Willie Dunn, who was laying out a golf course. Dunn teed up a few balls on a 125-yard par 3 which carried over a ravine and, after dropping them close to the pin, caused Vanderbilt to opine "this beats rifle shooting for distance and accuracy. It is a game I think would go over in our country." From this connection, two years later Dunn began the layout and construction of a 12-hole course at Shinnecock Hills, near the village of Southampton, Long Island.

Shortly after he finished the work at Shinnecock Hills, Dunn was retained by Marion's father and a group of neighbors to build a 9-hole course in Islip, a short distance from the South Side Club. The land they had selected had been developed into a grand estate two decades earlier by George Lorillard. Lorillard had been an avid ocean yacht racer until his schooner was wrecked in a gale off the African coast, and he was forced to pay the Bey of Tunis $15,000 ransom to obtain his freedom. Somewhat chastened, he turned his attention to horse racing, and built a track on his property.

Lorillard eventually sold his land to Bayard Cutting, and moved to Tuxedo Park. Cutting, in turn, provided the land needed for the Westbrook course. The routing crossed inside the race track and out, and also involved crossing the Long Island railroad tracks for two of the holes. Harry Hollins was elected the first president of the Westbrook Golf Club.

In the summer that Marion was five years old, the family spent a week at Sandwich, England. Playing a round at Royal St. George's, her father was assigned a young caddie named Arthur G. Griffiths. Returning to the course a few days later for another round, but alone, he was assigned Griffiths, this time as a partner to give him a match. Mr. Hollins liked the young man so much he invited him to come to America to be the golf professional at Westbrook. Griffiths accepted.

In those days when golf was less than ten years old in America, there were no mass-produced clubs. Griff, as he was universally known, had learned the craft of clubmaking at Royal St. George's, famous for its workmanship, and, before long, he was considered the best clubmaker in the United States.

At the club, Griff began a proper caddie program. Forty cents for the first nine, 35 for the second, with a 25-cent tip was the norm of the day, one caddie recalls, though some members didn't tip at all. If one of parsimonious fellows was spotted coming down the road, all the boys would dive into the adjacent corn field. Griff knew why they did, but he would stride into the cornstalks nonetheless, and flush one out.

Griff gave lessons as part of his duties, and it was he who began teaching Marion Hollins to play golf when she was six, a sport she was considered good at by age ten. He also taught her brothers, who went on to win many local tournaments. In fact, Griff was golf mentor to many of the Islip community, most of whom were excellent players. He always said that he could field a team of his players which could not be beaten.

In the histories of the early decades of golf in America, Marion's association with instruction in the sport is always tied to her introduction of Ernest Jones to this country. His influence on her and a generation of championship players is described in Chapter 9. It was Arthur Griffiths, however, who taught Marion her winning game. The first time she entered competitive golf, she not only qualified but almost won her first tournaments, including the United States Women's Amateur Championship. She never forgot her beginnings, and returned to Griff for years. Until she moved to the West Coast, Marion

*Arthur Griffiths, who taught Marion to play golf
at the Westbrook Golf Club.*

was always referred to in the press as "the girl from Westbrook,"
or "Miss Hollins of Westbrook." (The old course no longer exists as it has been absorbed partly by the Bayard Cutting
Aboretum and partly by the old Grumman aircraft facility.)

The game of golf expanded rapidly even though it was still
largely the sport of private clubs. The amateur tournaments

MISS MARION HOLLINS
Finish of a long drive.

*Illustration from an early book on women's golf instruction.
Marion Hollins about 22.*

were considered far more significant than the open champion-ship which included club professionals. In 1897, "just a few days before April Fools' Day, a group of what many would have considered eccentric middle-aged sportsmen gathered to dis-cuss the governance of a sport with which most Americans were unfamiliar" (from the centennial history of golf in the New York Metropolitan area). Shortly thereafter, the Metropolitan Golf Association was created, and Marion's father was elected its first president.*

Jumping ahead in history, in the early 1920s the men of Westbrook decided it was time to have an 18-hole course. The name of the new course was Timber Point, designed by the Brit-ish firm of golf architects, Colt and Allison. It was in its day considered one of the finest courses in the country. It took two years to complete. One hundred acres of land had to be created by draining wetlands through a series of embankments and sluices, and then dredging up sand from the Great South Bay, a scheme which would never be permitted today. Timber Point, par 71, 6,825 yards, had nine holes of pure seaside links among the dunes.

Marion, by this time, had captured the national Amateur Championship and was busy creating the Women's National Golf and Tennis Club on the North Shore. Although the illustrious golfer of the family, she was probably not much involved in the planning of Timber Point, but often played it on her later trips back east from California.

She was, however, indirectly responsible for the club's first professional, Angel de la Torre, a student of Ernest Jones, who she later installed at Pasatiempo as golf professional for the winter months.

Later dubbed the club of "the 50 bankrupt millionaires" because of the depression toll on some of its prominent founders, Timber Point membership was exclusive, and all the members belonged to the Suffolk County Republican Club. The presi-dent was W. Kingsland Macy. Harry Hollins, Jr., Marion's old-est brother, was chairman of the golf committee. Other members included Jay Carlisle, president of Seminole and a noted horse-

---

* The M.G.A. is one of the oldest and largest golf associations in this country, today representing over 400 golf clubs.

man and polo player: Horace Havemayer, Charles Lawrance, Landon Thorne, Marion's father, and other leaders of the Islip social set. Membership in Timber Point never reached 100, which was fine because the members liked their privacy.

When the county mosquito commission asked the club to contribute to an area-wide eradication of the pests, they were denied. The members preferred to keep the mosquitoes, fearing the increased traffic of people they imagined would arrive if the South Shore became known as a mosquito-free location. "The mosquitoes in the summer were unbelievable on that golf course," recalls Marion's nephew. "You'd look at the fellow you were playing with and there might be twenty on his face."

Timber Point had two memorable par 3s on the back nine links. The 12th, "Harbor," only 140 yards but played from an elevated tee to an elevated green with the yacht basin filling the entire space in between, required deadly accuracy. The most famous hole, "Gibraltar," was 200 yards uphill to a green atop a bluff whose sides fell away steeply to deep sand.

Timber Point still exists, but is now a county-owned greens-fee course, expanded to 27 holes, altering the layout. A golfer, however, can still experience much of the thrill of the old seaside holes that exist much as they were when Marion won the inaugural Long Island Championship trophy on this turf in 1927.

Coaching

Driving one, two, four, or even more horses pulling a rig of some sort was a necessity until, and into, the age of the automobile. Stagecoach, ice wagon, hay wagon, and beer wagon drivers all knew how to handle a team. Driving was also normal for gentlemen. They, however, were more likely to take the reins of a single horse or pair set to a light rig for a drive to the railroad station, or to visit a neighbor. When a larger rig and team was required, coachmen were used. In the 1870s, however, gentlemen began to enjoy coaching as a sport.

Four-in-hand driving, or tooling a coach, as it was called, was a fashionable activity in New York City for members of the Metropolitan and Knickerbocker Clubs. It became something of a craze to spend the day driving from New York City to some comfortable inn up the Hudson, lunching, and then making the return. More common than these longer runs were "parades" in which the teams were driven through Central Park, and then perhaps up to nearby Riverdale for refreshment.

As with most activities of the period, the etiquette of driving was specifically prescribed. Green coats with gilt buttons, silk top hats, a boutonniere, proper waistcoats, etc., were *de rigueur.* The hat was to be tipped on meeting another carriage the first time, whereas a nod sufficed at a second meeting, and so on. In addition to acquiring the skill involved in tooling a team, the owner of the coach made certain that the bright work was highly polished, and the tack in fine condition. Coachmen and grooms were in livery, and the horses decorated with bouquets of artificial flowers attached to their throat latches

The coach-and-four, not easy to control under the best of circumstances, was especially difficult to navigate in and around narrow city streets. The difficulty occurred in sharp turns. The lead pair tended to make the turn too abruptly, which then inclined the inward wheel pair to follow quickly. This resulted in pulling the coach into a corner building or other obstruction.

To handle these abrupt maneuvers, Maurice Howlett, son of the legendary instructor, trained his students, including Marion, in highly specific rein handling such as "bringing up the main wheel rein between the two lead reins and hanging it over the root of the thumb...." Like golf instruction, technique in the end must be sublimated to feel, but, also like golf, driving was an activity which took practice in order to become proficient.

Mrs. Thomas Hastings was the president of the Ladies' Four-in-Hand Club. Marion, a member and one of their leading whips, was cited in one publication as the *best* female driver of a coach-and-four. One of her favorite trips was from the Colony Club in New York City up the Hudson River to Tarrytown, where they ferried across, lunched at Nyack, and then went on to Tuxedo Park for the night before returning to the Colony the following day, a round-trip of approximately 100 miles.

There are newspaper and magazine photographs and descriptions of Marion taking a coach-and-four downtown New York City into Chinatown to test her skills in the narrow and twisting streets, a feat she accomplished "without ever touching a curbstone."

In a New York newspaper another testament to her driving abilities appears after World War I. Marion "drove Maurice

Marion Hollins tooling a coach in Paris at age 19.
Note the narrow street and sharp corner.

Howlett's coach 'Meteor' from the Hotel Astor to the new Brighton Beach Casino. Maurice Howlett who had instructed Marion Hollins from an early age was a professional whip. Meteor was considered one of the best appointed coaches in New York, and the trip was remarkable in that he never allowed amateurs to tool his coach and team."

Polo

She was one of the outstanding sports women of the world, was the only good woman polo player I have ever known.

—S.F.B. Morse in his unpublished
memoirs

Written after she died, this is a statement about Marion in her California years. Morse himself had been a great athlete at Yale, and was also an outstanding equestrian. The evaluation came from a practiced eye.

The origins of polo lie somewhere in central Asia, several hundred years before Christ. There are actual records of the game since 500 A.D. Modern polo came to the United States via Britain. It had evolved first in India among the horsemen of Manipur and then during the British Raj, when it became a sport among the many mounted officers. These gentlemen brought it back to England, where the various Lancers and Horse Guards added it to civilian pastimes.

If golf was essentially off-limits to women in its early years, polo was considered unthinkable for the fairer sex. In fact, polo was widely encouraged in the cavalry as a training and testing ground for combat. It is a game of "constant and real physical hazards," according to General George Patton. "No man can stay cool in battle unless he is habituated to the ex-hilarating sense of physical peril. No sport is so good in this respect as polo."

There was, however, a champion for the establishment of women's polo. Christened the mother of American polo for women, Louise Hitchcock instructed her children in the sport, and was a strong player as well. Her son, Thomas, would become the country's most famous player.

Mrs. Thomas Hastings, who had been instrumental in founding the Ladies' Four-in-Hand Driving Club, called a meeting at her home on the North Shore. The women present, including Mrs. Hitchcock and her two daughters, Celestine and Helen, were all expert horsewomen. The group decided to organize a schedule for female teams.

In the beginning they scrimmaged on fields on the Phipps and Bacon estates at Old Westbury, and on the Grace place in

*Marion Hollins in a practice polo scrimmage,
Del Monte, California.*

Great Neck. Soon, however, they were playing at the Meadow
Brook Club. One of Mrs. Hitchcock's teams, "The Meadow
Larks" was a male team, but Marion was invited to play with
them. In winter, many of these women continued the sport in
Aiken, South Carolina.

Golf Illustrated photo with caption: "Equestrians on the links at Aiken, S.C. Mr. J.E. Davis, a former Master of the Meadow Brook Hunt; Mrs. J.E. Davis, a noted horsewoman; Mr. Oakleigh Thorne, master of the Millbrook Hunt; and Miss Marion Hollins, as well known in the hunting field as upon the links."

A polo team consists of four players, the forward two being the primary goal scorers, number four being a defensive position, and number three prepared to defend or attack. In her day, Marion played all the positions, and in the 1930s was captain of the team that defeated the well-known Riviera team for the California's Governor's Cup.

A man's handicap rating in polo is established by a goal count, 10 goal being the highest, –2 representing the lowest level at which there is an acknowledged rating. According to newspaper articles, Marion was the only woman in America to have been awarded a man's handicap.

In the 1930s as women began fielding more and more teams, a handicap system was created for them, 8 being the top level. In 1936 at age 44, overweight and well past her prime, Marion nonetheless earned a 6-goal rating. (Her rating on the men's scale was 2.)

Polo is considered a dangerous activity for player and horse alike. As Marion was fearless—that quality is noted by commentaries in the press of the day *ad nauseum*—that she loved the game is no surprise. But the horses....

Polo is an expensive sport. First, the training of a good polo pony is a long process. Second, because of the physical requirements of the game, a pony has to quickly accelerate to a full gallop, make abrupt and violent changes in direction, and is frequently in physical contact with other horses. Thus, a player needs many horses within a single game, and good players maintain a string of polo ponies. As a consequence, players do not normally lend out their steeds. Marion was a stunning exception. Two of the top ranking players of the world, Thomas Hitchcock and Harry Payne Whitney, both inducted into the Polo Hall of Fame, were happy to loan her their horses.

In her teenage years and until she moved west in 1924 at age 32, Marion was a frequent commuter from East Islip on the South Shore to Meadow Brook and Piping Rock on the North Shore for her games of polo. And even at Meadowfarm, friends would gather for informal chukkers and impromptu steeplechase challenges.

Strange as it seems today, when Marion entered tournament golf in 1912, and was runner-up in the Metropolitan Golf Association Championship, the newspapers of the day identified her as "the well known horsewoman and polo player."

Chapter Five

Marion Hollins
Comes of Age

*A*s a member of an old-guard family, Marion "was introduced to society" as a debutante in 1908. She would have attended all the cotillions, dinners, teas, and parties that were a part of the social scene. Although there is no indication that religion played much of a role in her life, she was baptized and confirmed in the Episcopal Church, and her mother noted in a scrapbook that she took her first communion in December, 1910.

We know that Marion went to Europe almost every summer prior to World War I. In 1914, she spent five winter weeks at Aiken with Gertrude Vanderbilt. As the latter was then married to Harry Payne Whitney, a 10-goal polo player, and Louise Hitchcock was there as well, we can assume they were playing a good deal of polo.

Such were the normal activities of a young woman of the leisure class in the early 1900s. Marion, however, was never defined by the expected.

The Flame of Kapur

The motion picture industry was in its infancy in 1914, and it would be years before sound would be added. One center of the industry was a company called Vitagraph in Brooklyn. A group from Islip decided to make a feature film to be produced by Vitagraph. It was titled *The Flame of Kapur,* "a lurid melodrama, as were most movies in that day," according to Schuyler Parsons. Marion played one of the leads. Her scenes included a fox hunt at Meadow Brook, a golf tournament, and an automobile race along the Vanderbilt track. The film won rave reviews in the papers, and "the audience jammed the Waldorf ballroom for a week" to see it, movie theaters then being few and far between. Unfortunately, early films were seldom preserved, and there is no record that *The Flame of Kapur* is still in existence.

The National Horse Show

In 1917 Marion was a principal in one of the most august horsing events ever held, the National Horse Show.

"The aristocracy of the horse domain held court in grand style in Madison Square Garden last night, while a vast crowd of society and horse lovers gazed with admiration on the animated picture of equine beauty in the tanbark ring," reported the *New York Times.*

It was the largest show in over 30 years, and the Garden was appropriately decorated. The ceiling and walls were covered with swaths of red and white cloth. The boxes were decorated with red geraniums and clinging vines. The entrance for the riders was hidden by a forest of fully grown evergreens.

Opening night commenced with a fanfare of trumpets. A bugler announced the class of ladies' jumpers. Representing the Meadow Brook Hunt were Mrs. Thomas Hitchcock, Helen Hitchcock, and Marion Hollins riding Harry Payne Whitney's "Moonblossom." The papers reported it as the most spectacular event of the evening, abounding "in feats of horsemanship."

The night's concluding event was the Alfred G. Vanderbilt Gold Challenge Cup for driving. One of the two entering teams had withdrawn, however, and only one contestant was expected to enter the ring. A great roar of applause filled the Garden when, unexpectedly, a second coach and four, Alfred Vanderbilt's team of grays driven by Marion, sped into the ring, the coachman playing "The Sidewalks of New York" on his horn. The teams were not in formal competition as the decision to have Marion drive as an added attraction had been made at the last moment. Nonetheless, it was a treat for the spectators to see the two greatest teams of grays in the country being tooled by the two greatest drivers.

Each day of the week-long National Horse Show, Marion tooled a team from the Colony Club to Madison Square Gar-

*Marion Hollins tooling a coach and four down
Fifth Avenue in New York City in 1917.*

den. The coach was the famous "Arrow" which had belonged
to the Ladies' Four-in-Hand Driving Club. The horses were the
renowned grays of the late Alfred Gwynne Vanderbilt,* noted
as "probably the fastest trotters ever shown to coach."

The New York papers all carried photographs of Marion
Hollins's arrival at the Garden. Each day her coach was filled
with paying passengers as a contribution to the Red Cross. On

---

* Alfred Vanderbilt had been a well-known sporting figure and used
to drive one of his elegant coaches, "Viking" and "Venture," on 5th
Avenue and in Central Park. He was aboard the *Lusitania* when she
was torpedoed. Handing his life jacket to a woman, he told his
valet, "Save all the kiddies you can."

Vanderbilt and his valet both perished. A survivor recalled, "He
stood there, the personification of sportsmanlike coolness. In my
eyes he was the figure of a gentleman waiting for a train."

Martial Hue to Horse Show Opening; Red Cross Dominates All at Garden

ARMY STEEDS EXHIBITED BY OFFICERS

Finest Saddle Horses and Trotters Shown, and Peter Hauck, Jr.'s, Pony Mare, My Nora, Wins the First Blue Ribbon of the Day

OLIVE DRAB mingled with the red and white yesterday at the opening of the thirty-second annual Horse Show at Madison Square Garden. Subdued by martial hues were the gay colors beloved by sportsmen.

Khaki and military bugles took the place of the whip and spur. Men in khaki and men in naval blue thronged the audience, and army officers exhibited their steeds of war. Society women, watching the horses prance around the tan-bark ring from their boxes, were knitting busily the things our soldiers need.

In and out among the throngs moved women wearing the white uniform of red cross nurses. Their red hoods bobbed gaily in and out among the crowds. The women in Red Cross uniforms were ushering the spectators to their seats.

The war time spirit has New York in its grip, and the war time spirit has taken this year's Horse Show by storm. It is being held this year for the benefit of the Red

MISS MARION HOLLINS *driving famous gray four-in-hand owned by the late Alfred G. Vanderbilt from the Colony Club to Madison Square Garden.*

---

one day the passengers included William H. Moore, a famous whip; Joseph E. Davis, Master of Foxhounds at Meadow Brook; and Helen Hitchcock. And on the final day, in the coach were Marion's good friends, the great Boston athlete, Eleanora Sears of Boston, and Mr. and Mrs. Ambrose Clark and Mr. Henry Worthington Bull, "after taking tea at the Colony."

Vanderbilt [Automobile Race] Cup

Any reference book or article which includes even a brief biographical notation on Marion Hollins includes the fact that she was the first woman to enter an automobile race, and that the race was the Vanderbilt Cup. It makes sense because she was friends with the family, and the event was a social one.

Two of Marion's nieces confirm that Marion did in fact drive a car in the Vanderbilt Cup. I have been unable to document the year in which she did so, but as press coverage was mostly focused on the winners and well-known names, as well as lurid descriptions of the grisly scenes, this does not discount the family's recollection and historical references.

America's first automobile race got underway on Long Island just after dawn on an autumn day in 1904. The Waldorf-Astoria Hotel had catered 52 society breakfast parties heading for the races, and there were an extraordinary 25,000 spectators on hand to witness the inaugural Vanderbilt Cup Race. This was a big event, and was a preview of the enormous audiences automobile racing has attracted ever since.

The 284-mile race was routed over public roads, and much of it was through farming country. It turned out to be a bloody spectacle. One driver mistakenly ran over his own mechanic. Residents along the route were advised to keep their children indoors, and "cautioned against allowing domestic animals or fowl to be at large." Spectators who had never before seen an automobile race not only lined the road but walked out on it to see what was coming.

In Brooklyn a minister railed from the pulpit, "Men of to-day are choking themselves with luxuries. Oh, the degradation of such a scene! As foolish as a bullfight; as vulgar as reddening the sands in a gladiatorial contest; as revolting as bartering Christ's garments for a few pieces of silver."

But of course the first race was only an advertisement for the second running of the Cup. Even larger crowds lined the road. Vendors sold little sticks with feathers attached to the end so that spectators could try to tickle the drivers as they hurtled by.

Ken Purdy wrote in the *Atlantic Monthly,* "'I tickled Lancia,' a woman would scream. 'That's nothing,' another would answer her, 'I got Nazzaro on the last round!'.... The races of '04 and '05 were mere warm-ups for 1906. The running of the Cup that year provided sport on a truly Homeric scale...."

The race was now attracting a crowd in excess of 300,000, and accidents began to take their toll among the spectators as automobiles plowed into them. In one accident the driver crashed into a farmhouse, propelling his mechanic through the air to his death, whereupon his body was immediately stripped naked by souvenir-seeking spectators. Because of the carnage, no race was held in 1907, but it was on again in 1908. Drivers, now, were cautioned not to drink so much champagne before the start.

1910 was the last year the race was held in Long Island. Four people dead and more than a score in the hospital was too much. The crowd of a half million, many inebriated, trampled at least one observer to death. Thereafter the race would be held in other cities around the country.

In the 1930s the Cup, given by William K. Vanderbilt, Jr., was retired and given to the Smithsonian. It had been made by Tiffany, had a capacity of 10½ gallons, and contained 481 ounces of sterling silver.

Chapter Six

Champion

Away out there in the dim and distant future, when the stars of a coming day shall turn to gaze on the records of days that are past and to listen to the prattling of the veterans who call on memory to conjure up deeds of bygone days, golfers are going to refer to 1921 as one remarkable for a long list of notable achievements—a year that saw the eclipse of favorites of long standing and the ascendancy of new luminaries to the links firmament.... And finally they'll tell you of how Marion Hollins survived through the deadliest struggle that ever marked the contest for the Women's Championship of the United States to win the 1921 title.

With that rather melodramatic opening paragraph, the *American Golfer* began its reportage of the 1921 Women's National Championship played at the Hollywood course in Deal, New Jersey. The tournament began with 181 entries in a qualifying medal-play round from which the top 36 went on to the championship. Included in this field were some golfers heavily favored to win. Alexa Stirling from Atlanta had turned back all challengers to her supremacy since 1916. From England came Cecil Leitch, the British and Canadian champion, and her sister, Edith. Marion, now 29, had been stalking the title for almost a decade.

In 1912, at the age of 20, she had entered competitive golf, qualifying in the Metropolitan Golf Association championship, in which she went to the finals. The M.G.A. included players from courses in New York, New Jersey, and Connecticut which lay within 55 miles of New York City.

All of these tournaments began with a qualifying round for the aspirants. It was based on stroke play, and the player with the low score was known as Medalist. Then the top qualifiers entered the tournament proper, which was based on match play. The number of slots in a tournament varied from year to year.

In 1913, after winning the Metropolitan Golf Association trophy, Marion made her first challenge in the United States Women's Amateur Championship. After three rounds she found herself in the semifinals against Miss Harriet Curtis of Essex, Massachusetts, who, with her sister, would later donate the Curtis Cup (see Chapter 15). Marion squeaked out a victory on the 20th hole from the former champion, and then it was on to the finals.

There she met the great English player Gladys Ravenscroft, who had won her country's championship the prior year, for the deciding 36-hole contest.* Marion lost on the home green, but need not have done so. Twice when her opponent was in trouble and Marion was already on the green, she failed to sink the putt in one, failed to two-putt, failed to get down in three. Those two four-putt holes cost her the championship, and led to a reputation which lingered on that, while perhaps the longest woman golfer off the tee, she was indifferent in her putting.

In 1914, Marion played well in the qualifier but lost in the first round to her Long Island neighbor and friend, Lillian Hyde. In 1915 she again qualified, but lost to the Philadelphia player Mrs. Barlow. She suffered another first round loss in 1916. In 1919 she lost in the second round to the defending champion and eventual winner, Alexa Stirling.

In 1920 Marion shattered the Medalist record, scoring *four strokes* lower than the lowest score ever posted in a qualifying round, but again lost, this time in the quarter-finals.

In the spring of 1920, Marion went to Europe with a small contingent of U.S. and Canadian golfers. The site of the British Ladies' Championship (it was always "Ladies'" there, "Women's" here) was Royal County Down, Newcastle, Ireland.

---

* It is interesting today, with all the comments on the physical strains of an 18-hole match vs riding a cart, to note that the final matches of all the women's tournaments were 36 holes with a break for lunch after the first 18.

*Marion Hollins in finish of a full swing at the 1913 Women's
National Championship. She was runner-up.*

Rain, gales, and blowing sand were the conditions. Marion
won her first three rounds over the leading players from Walton
Heath, Sunningdale, and Royal Portrush. She was defeated in
the fourth round by Molly Griffiths, the eventual runner-up.

The players she had just met in Ireland invited her back to
England for the summer, but Marion headed first for Paris. In a
note to her mother she wrote that she hoped to spend August
in Deauville with her parents, then the chic French summer
resort in Normandy. She ends by adding "Bob J. in the finals
today. It is too exciting. I hope he wallops Tolley. I could live
here for 40 francs a day with meals. That is $3 and a bath with
it. Love, Marion."

While in Europe, Marion entered the Ladies' Championship of France, held that year at Le Touquet. In her first round
she defeated Miss E.E. Helme, famous for her putting skills,
on the home green. When she reached the semifinals she lost
to Molly Griffiths, who once again lost in the finals to Cecil
Leitch.

Marion Hollins at the 1913 Women's
National Championship.

*Marion Hollins with Mrs. Clarence Vanderbeck, Miss Mildred
Caverly, and Miss Rosamond Sherwood boarding a liner
to challenge at the British Ladies' Championship.*

And so, with her game in shape, Marion ended 1920 in high
spirits, having competed well against Europe's top players as
well as setting a record at home. What else she did with her
days while overseas we will never know. Contemporary magazines made references to Marion Hollins having played polo
with members of the crack British men's team which challenged
America at Piping Rock. We can assume, therefore, that part of
her summer was spent on horseback on the polo field and riding
to the hounds.

The following year, 1921, the U.S. championship was scheduled for October, so there was plenty of time for Marion to sail
back to England for the British Ladies' Championship Tournament at Turnberry. All attention to the contingent of U.S. play-

American Golfer *1924 analysis of*
Marion Hollins's full swing.

ers centered on Alexa Stirling, who had won the last three national titles at home. The great speculation was on what would
happen if the U.S. champion should meet Cecil Leitch, her
British counterpart, somewhere in the pairings. In the luck of
the draw, they met in the first round. The match was played in
fierce weather with sheets of rain driving across the Turnberry

links on the back of gale-force winds. Even so, a crowd of several thousand was on hand to watch Leitch win the match. And who should the victorious Leitch meet in the second round, but Marion, having won her own match the previous day.

The pair teed off at 12:15 in a strong wind. Cecil Leitch was soon forced to take note that the reputation of Marion's weak putting was amiss. Writing about the match afterward, she noted, "The chief recollect I have of that match is that my opponent holed out in one putt with the most astonishing regularity."

On the 17th tee Marion was one up with two to play, but sliced her drive. Watching its disastrous flight she remarked to herself out loud, "Fernie told me not to jump on my left toe, and I've remembered all the time until just now."

She lost the hole and they arrived at the 18th all square. Marion's second shot landed short of the green in a bunker. Cecil Leitch was on the green. Marion played her shot to the pin, but the ball rolled back into the bunker. Her second attempt also failed. At that point "my cheery opponent," as Cecil Leitch characterized her, left the bunker and walked across the green to shake her opponent's hand. Cecil Leitch went on to win the British Ladies' National title over the legendary Joyce Wethered.

Back home, Marion was putting the finishing touches to her game. She returned from England just in time to enter the qualifying round for the Griswald Cup Challenge at the Shennecossett Country Club near New London, Connecticut. It was a strong field. In the second round Marion defeated Miss Frances Griscom, the 1900 National Champion. In the semifinals she met Mrs. William Gavin of Bellclaire, New Jersey, the 1915 finalist. The combination of tremendous drives and the psychological advantage from birdieing the 538-yard 13th hole brought victory to Marion on the 16th hole.

The final match was between Marion and Mrs. Arnold Jackson, winner of the Metropolitan Golf Association title in 1920. (In 1919 Marion had won this title, but did not defend it the following year as she was abroad.) Marion won the match.

The tournament was a good example of Marion's great length working to advantage. Heavy rains had left the course soft. Lesser hitters were unable to get a roll onto the putting surface, while Marion was reaching greens with her second shot all by carry. "She was a powerful player," wrote Rhonda Glenn, "and her emergence as champion inspired other American women to try and hit longer tee shots. Glenna Collett, for one, modeled part of her game after Miss Hollins' example and wrote that Marion was one of the five longest drivers in women's golf."

Marion stayed on at Shennecossett in order to take some lessons from Alec (or Alex) Smith, its head professional. Smith deserves a brief digression. He emigrated to the United States from Carnoustie, Scotland, and his first work was as a greenskeeper and clubmaker in Chicago. In 1901 he moved to the Nassau Country Club in Long Island, and in 1906 won the U.S. Open for the first of two times.

Mentor to the great turn-of-the-century amateur champion, Jerome D. Travers, Smith became the guiding influence to the sixteen-year-old Rhode Islander, Glenna Collett. Before she rested her clubs, Glenna won six U.S. championships, and was victorious in major tournaments more than *any* golfer—male or female—with 49 wins in 18 years.

Smith was known for being short on praise and without sympathy. He prided himself on never, within earshot, commenting favorably on a player, including the likes of the colorful many-time champion, Walter Hagen. Aside from his champions, Smith also helped weekend golfers straighten out their slice, and was active with young children just taking up the game. Considered the fastest player in golf, he was nicknamed "miss 'em quick Smith" for his rapid putting.

Smith was equally fast with repartee. Only once was he struck with a loss for words. He had become frustrated with the lack of progress he was obtaining from a large lady to whom he had been giving one-hour lessons daily for a month, sometimes in both morning and afternoon.

"I gie up, lassie," he told her, "it's nae use because you'll never make a gowfer in this world." To which she replied, "I don't want to be a golfer, Mr. Smith. I never even said I did. I am only taking lessons to reduce." Alec looked at her, speechless, then strode off the practice range and left the course for the rest of the day.

Armed with Alec Smith's fine-tuning, Marion Hollins arrived for the National Championship at the Hollywood course in Deal, New Jersey. The course contained severe bunkering (37 on one hole alone), undulations in the fairways, and "[the pins cut] on alarming slopes. The most difficult I have yet seen and one of the longest I have ever played over," claimed Cecil Leitch. One of the favorites, Edith Cummings, failed even to qualify, taking a 12 on the 510-yard 10th hole after being unable to exit a bunker in which she lay 3.

Many other forceful contenders lost in the early rounds. Glenna Collett, the Medalist, was eliminated early on by Cecil

*Marion Hollins and Alexa Stirling after the former wins
the 1921 Women's National Championship.
Stirling had reigned since 1916.*

Leitch, who in turn was defeated in an upset by Mrs. F.C. Letts, who proceeded to lose the next day to Marion.

In the semifinals, Marion defeated her opponent on the 19th hole. Alexa Stirling, the defending champion, won her match on the 18th.

In the finals, Marion was 3 up against Alexa at the turn, and 4 up after 18. They stopped for lunch during which a bone-chilling, wind-driven downpour spread across the course. The pair set off on the final 18 in fierce conditions. Alexa won two of the first four holes, and the gallery began to sense that she might be on her way to another victory. The contender rallied, however, and was again 4 up with 9 holes to play.

At this point, Marion had steadied and was now grinding out workmanlike golf. Alexa must have felt inwardly that she was in a losing fight. She won the difficult 10th, but then came the 11th. At so many tournaments, or just as likely at a local Sunday morning match between two friends, comes a shot which saps the spirit of a struggling opponent. Alexa Stirling experienced it on the 11th.

Marion had sent her drive long but far left. Alexa had the shorter drive, so played her second shot first. It was a mishit. Her third shot found a greenside bunker. Now Marion had a choice: she could play safe by sending the ball into the fairway short of the green, then onto the green in three, down in not more than two. However, if Alexa could get up and down from the bunker, she would halve the hole.

Marion Hollins was in the rough, the pin hidden by a line of trees extending out from the left side of the course. Although she could not see it, she knew that the flag was near the middle of the green. She took an iron from her bag and sent the ball curving around the end of the tree line in a slight hook. The ball landed on the green and stopped near its middle. Although it was still possible for Alexa to make a recovery, in fact Marion had won the match. It ended on the 14th, 5 and 4.

Chapter Seven

Just Plain Old Fun at the Game of Golf

$\mathcal{S}$carcely had the 1921 championship been secured than an exhibition match was arranged, pitting Marion and Mrs. William A. Gavin against Edith and Cecil Leitch at Baltusrol in New Jersey. The new U.S. Champion and her partner won on the 18th green.

Marion wanted to show the overseas visitors all the courses she loved in her home country. Cecil Leitch later commented that Americans seemed to think nothing of motoring 10 or 12 hours to get in an interesting round of golf. Of course she was in Marion's hands, which may explain something. "Oh, it's nothing. It's just overnight," she laughed.

Then as autumn changed the color of the landscape, it was time to visit Long Island. In the first match on Marion's home turf, Cecil Leitch and Rosamond Sherwood were trounced by Edith Leitch and Marion, "the National Champion converting what promised to be a particularly close match into a veritable farce.... On two greens in this match [Marion] holed putts of 25 *yards* for wins, and what is more, the ball never looked like missing the hole from the instant it was hit," wrote Cecil Leitch, in her autobiography, *Golf.*

Marion loved to bring her British friends to play the National Links at Southampton. That year, Cecil's last game in America was on the famous course, a match of Marion and Cecil against Devereux Emmet and the Staten Island champion, Mr. Follett. The women were considered serious underdogs, but Marion told her partner that this course always had an inspiring impact on her game. True to Marion's expectation, though 2 down after 12 holes, the women turned the game around and won the match 2 up.

In her autobiography, Cecil Leitch looked back on Marion as "a most delightful companion and gifted with a keen sense of humor. Nothing is a trouble to Miss Hollins and she will undertake a long journey for a round of golf which few would consider worthwhile. No one is more appreciative of the good features of a course, a quality which makes her an interesting and satisfying partner or opponent. For many reasons I shall never forget that day's golf over the National Links on Long Island, but it is chiefly impressed upon my memory as that on which Miss Hollins completed the homeward half in a score of 37, likely to stand as a ladies' record for many years."

It is a few years earlier. January 1st, 1917, Long Island. Winter. Snow. Golf courses closed. Well, *officially* closed. But wait: there is a tournament about to begin. Are we witnessing a New Year's Day challenge between the two clubs of Piping Rock and Nassau? Of course.

The New Year's Day's play will start with a few holes at Nassau, then cross the railroad, past the barn of Marion Hollins's relative, H. Coles, through Congressman Cocks's estate, across other private lands, then by the Quaker Meeting House, skirting—if possible—some corn fields, down the Piping Rock Club racetrack, and finally to the home hole up by the clubhouse.

Caddies were posted along the entire route to flag errant balls in snowbanks, backyards, and gutters. A field of 43 men and 11 women showed up for this extreme golf.

On this particular New Year's Day in Long Island, the mixed doubles prize went to Howard F. Whitney and Marion Hollins, whose scores were 26 and 30 on the nutty 4,000 yard course. Press coverage of this unique game noted that "Miss Hollins put to blush the misguided efforts of many male golfers. Only eight improved on her score."

Golf in America, it must be remembered, was making up for lost time since its discovery. Why else, for example, would society head for Lake Placid in winter to play a round of golf in snowshoes, after a morning of skijoring?

In 1941 in another remarkable round, Marion entered the women's championship tournament at Cypress Point. Out of a field of 40 entries, only four finished, with Marion the champion. On the final day of the tournament, torrential rains triggered by mid-winter cyclonic movements over the Pacific descended onto the Monterey coast. The drenching downpour never abated. Marion and her fellow competitors played on. One of the foursome, Mildred Yorba MacArthur, described the afternoon:

"It was Marion who shot the golf that day. She never lost her swing for an instant, because she didn't try to keep from getting wet, like the rest of us. She wore no hat, windbreaker, scarf, or other hindrances that the rest of us resorted to. Instead, she wore two slipover cashmere sweaters, and now and then she'd stop and wring them out, laughing heartily as the water poured into her already soaked shoes.

"Her beloved dog, 'Ganz' started out with us. At the third hole she looked back and saw the miserable creature making his way through the downpour. She spotted a workman nearby and called to him, asking him if he'd mind taking the dog to the clubhouse in his vehicle. As she carried him to the back of the pickup she said, 'This is no kind of weather for a dog to be out gallerying.' It wasn't, but we learned a lot of golf that day.

"She used a two iron for almost every shot, including putting on the flooded greens. She allowed as much as forty or fifty feet for wind drifts as she started her shots out, that ultimately found their way to the greens. Marion shot a heroic 91 that day, while the rest of us went well over the hundred mark, and still finished in the money."

Golf, golf, golf. If you are going to do it, do it. In 1921 Marion established a tradition of taking full advantage of a British links course when she and some companions went out after dinner at Turnberry. In the long evening shadows, carrying their own bags, they played a round into the gloaming, the night before the Ladies' Championship.

It is nine years later, and again on the morrow the Ladies' Championship is about to begin, this time at St. Andrews. But what to do this evening before the tournament? At the venerable ladies' putting club alongside the first fairway sits one of the most challenging 18-hole putting courses, known as the Himalayas—a miniature tract of bumpy links land. Marion decided to host a putting party, with a unique set of rules. The female contestants, champions all, were required to putt in a variety of novel club and body positions. On one shot, Marion had to lie down and, as in billiards, cue the ball into the hole.

Wrote Eleanor Helme, one of the players, "She would be a daring correspondent who revealed what might have been seen as this lady of ample proportions [carried out the assignment].

"At St. Andrews it may be possible to joke about the choice of a career, going to a funeral, getting married. But to joke about golf! Reduce the playing of it to a subject of mirth, what were golfers coming to? The answer was that the golfers had come to St. Andrews determined to enjoy every minute of a unique experience. The waters of the Swilcan could float by, carrying the hopes of many to their grave in the ocean. Miss Hollins' putting party would have its laugh."

(Marion lost in the fourth match, but was comforted by a telegram she received at her hotel. "Grass is peeking through the soil at Santa Cruz," it read. Pasatiempo was becoming a reality.)

However it was not always golf above all. In one Metropolitan Golf Association Championship the lead players were Marion from Long Island, Glenna Collett from Connecticut, and Maureen Orcutt from New Jersey. As such, they had the honors of being the last threesome to tee off. On the way to the competition Maureen's auto got a flat tire and, by the time they started, they were well behind the rest of the field. "We have to play quickly," Marion told her competitors. "I need to be at a polo match."

Starting well last, the three played through every group in the tournament and were the first to finish.

Chapter Eight

The Women's National Golf and Tennis Club

During the 1920s and early 1930s, the forceful personality of Marion Hollins galvanized the early tremors of feminism in women's golf. A strong performer on the amateur circuit who won the 1921 U.S. Women's Amateur Championship, Miss Hollins, more than many champions, stands out.... In 1923, just three years after women won the right to vote, Marion Hollins ramrodded the organizing of the Women's National Golf and Tennis Club on Long Island.

—Rhonda Glenn, *The Illustrated History of Women's Golf*

No woman golfer has done more for the game of golf in America than Miss Marion Hollins.

—H.B. Martin, 1936, in *50 Years of American Golf*

*W*omen had been playing golf in the United States almost since its inception late in the 1880s. They were, however, hardly tolerated. Unlike the Scottish links where the course lay on common land and the "club house" might be no more than a shed, the early days of golf in the United States evolved around privately subscribed courses with elegant facilities. They were exclusionary, redoubts of privilege, and at some the gates were closed even to the wives of members.

This, in turn, led to the factually based expression "golf widow." Women stayed at home while the men spent their summer hours at the club either playing golf or sitting around discussing their golf. This amusing bit of doggerel by Russell Hobson was published as Marion Hollins was moving to the top ranks of amateur golf.

"Who's the stranger, Mother Dear?
Look! He knows us! Ain't he queer?"

"Hush My Own! Don't talk so wild;
That's your father, dearest child."

"That's my father? No such thing!
Father died, you know, last spring."

"Father didn't die, you dub!
Father joined a golfing club.

"But they closed the club, so he
Had no place to go, you see—

"No place left for him to roam.
That's why he's coming home...

"Kiss him, he won't bite you, Child!
All those golfing guys look wild."

"A woman's place is in the home" was a maxim of the day (only slightly less discriminatory than Calvin Coolidge's quip that "a woman's place is in the wrong," which at least was intended to be funny). Women who ventured into the game of golf were nicknamed "golferines." Men clearly preferred that the ladies grace the club verandas in pretty frocks and boaters, if they had to be there at all. Glenna Collett in her autobiography recalls, about women and golf: "Amused men felt they were too flighty to concentrate seriously on the game." And Herbert Warren Wind, dean of U.S. golf writers noted that the husbands did not want their wives playing golf because the sport "developed unbecoming muscles."

Etiquette of the day decreed that dress was a serious matter. Men were fortunate. Prescribed outfits for their sporting events were at least tailored to accommodate the activity, not to mention their natural, male biological shapes. Women did not fare as well. Enid Wilson, champion woman golfer and an ardent feminist, recalled, "The hour-glass was the desired form of the women of fashion in the 1890s...and having constricted their middles, the ladies then proceeded to add drapes, such as puffed sleeves and voluminous skirts. The wonder was that they ever did anything.... Many women [golfers] had their skirts bound with leather at the bottom, to prevent the material from fraying as it trailed on the ground; the binding could be sponged to wipe off mud collected on the way around. Collars and ties—high, stiff, starched collars and club ties—were also an important part of the uniform."

Female interest in golf was increasing, however, and something had to be done. Some clubs built an adjacent course of a few holes for women's enjoyment. Or, women were allowed on the course at off-hours on selected weekdays. Having made some accommodations, golf clubs remained a bastion of male supremacy.

In spite of the limitations, an article in the *American Golfer* calculated in 1920 that there were twelve women who could give nine strokes to 250,000 male golfers and win; 500 who could play even and beat 300,000; and 50,000 who could hold their own "with the class C (the largest category) of players who are the committeemen who keep them out, out even from practice."

There was an additional problem for women golfers. Courses designed by men for men were not perfectly suited to a woman's game.

Differences in physique produce a natural differential in the distances that, on average, the two sexes can drive a ball from the tee. And many are the par 4s which require a drive of well over 200 yards if par is to be threatened. The difference is, perhaps, greater between the mid-to-high handicap players than at the championship level. However, in the case of the scratch player, the average difference between men and women still remains at about 30 yards. Therefore, before women's tees were established, on a typical par 4, a man's second shot into the green was with an iron that had some loft, permitting a ball to land on the green and stop. Women, on the other hand, playing from the same tees, usually needed to hit a wood for their approach shot, with its built-in decreased accuracy and stopping power.

This was of no concern to the men. Women were, after all, the "weaker sex," an attitude that died slowly, and maybe is not yet entirely in the grave.

Laura Curtis, niece of Margaret and Harriet Curtis, and herself a qualifier for the U.S. Amateur, was a disciple of Ernest Jones, and knew the Women's National Golf and Tennis Club and its history. An advocate of women's tees, she once told Ben Hogan that "on some of the long par 4s [from the men's tees] I had to hit a drive, a brassie, and a pitch to reach the green. He looked at me and said, 'Why don't you go fishing instead?'"

However, in the earlier time of Marion's day, men were slowly but gradually coming to the realization that women were not only very serious about golf but were even challenging them to matches. The male establishment decided that the difference between the scores of the two sexes rested at about 10 strokes a round, and it became the norm for a man to give a woman nine strokes. Most idiotically, the formula was to give a stroke on every other hole, without regard to whether the hole was a par 3, a long or short par 4.

In the 1920s this random allocation of strokes was replaced by the use of "bisques," a handicapping system no longer in existence, but a good one, nonetheless. A bisque was a stroke which could be used at any hole upon the conclusion of play at that hole. At a level of scratch play a man would give a woman six bisques. Thus, for example, if each made par at a short hole, the woman could use a bisque, and win with a net two. Or if she shot bogey to a man's par, she could halve the hole, electing to use one of her bisques.

This made a contest more fair, but did nothing to alter the fact that golf courses were laid out based on the average length of a man's drive.

Into this scene came Marion Hollins after winning the United States Women's Amateur Championship. Early in 1922 she assembled a group of women and broached an idea she had formulated: why not build a championship course designed *for* women? This would not be one of the toy layouts that men built for them, but a course that would challenge the best woman golfer, yet not completely overpower the average female player.

"It is impossible for most women players to compete with a man's course on equal terms with par or even bogey, " she wrote. "[I decided] to make a course which would bring out the best in women's golf, without sacrificing length or hazards."

The concept in place, who was to find the land, plan, finance, and organize the membership? Why, women. And the membership in the new club would be limited to women. Men could play at the facility—just as long as they were invited and were accompanied by one of the women who were members. It would be called the Women's National Golf and Tennis Club.

Marion divided the initial subscribers into working groups. The most immediate assignments were to find a suitable piece of land, and to finance the acquisition. Marion herself, armed with a camera and a small motion picture outfit, then departed for Britain to scout out courses for holes that fit her definition of a woman's national course. This concept of adapting exemplary holes had been used to great effect by Charles Blair Macdonald at the National Golf Links in Southampton, Long Island. Marion had played the course often, and her father was one of the founding members.

She had no end of contacts on the other side of the Atlantic. Cecil Leitch, with whom she had competed many times, helped her, as did other leading amateurs and professionals. For example, she played and discussed Walton Heath with James Braid, six-time winner of the British championship. In short order, she played over 20 courses, making notes and sketches, and taking photographs and movies all the while.

"Looking well and energetic after her [return] voyage, and with her brown eyes dancing with enthusiasm," she turned over the material to Devereux Emmet who, assisted by Seth Raynor and Macdonald in the final stages, was to design the actual layout.

The hilly land, which had been bought in Glen Head, Long Island, offered a beautiful site for a course with many elevation changes. "It was the best, in my opinion, that could have been chosen, and its fine rolling qualities will undoubtedly appeal to the golfing eye," she wrote for *Golf Illustrated* in a long essay on her philosophy of golf course design.

Thanks to her survey of courses in Britain, several holes at the Women's National Golf and Tennis Club were either mirrors, or adaptations, of exemplary holes she had seen. The first hole was reminiscent of the 7th hole at the new course at Walton Heath, and the 4th a copy of the 11th at Northampton. "The Principal's Nose at St. Andrews finds a very good imitation in the seventeenth, a hole of about three hundred and seventy-five yards, with two or three alternate ways of playing," Marion wrote. The 12th hole at the Women's National was "fashioned after the famous third hole at Mid-Surrey."

She and Devereux Emmet also looked for inspiration at courses in Long Island. The 5th hole was very similar to the 5th at her home course, Westbrook; the 8th an adaptation of the 5th at the National; and the 11th was close to the 13th at Piping Rock.

Lastly, she liked the small grassy hills near the greens found in the links courses of the British Isles. Similar hummocks were incorporated as was the option of a run-up play on most holes. This was not links land, but Marion loved those seaside courses and their receptivity to that shot.*

---

* In his autobiography, Alister MacKenzie writes about Saunton on the west coast of England. "It is magnificent sand dune country.... It has, however, the distinction of having been criticized in no uncertain terms by the majority of the American Women's Golf Team. Their captain, Marion Hollins, was an exception, but she knows and has played on real sand dune courses so frequently that she has learned to appreciate their virtues."

The 16th hole at the Women's National Golf and Tennis Club.
Note the British influence on the sculpting of the green and the bunker.

In a short time, the Women's National Golf and Tennis Club had over 300 members, well on its way to the predetermined limit of 400.

Meanwhile, Marion had had to answer the central question of the entire project. What *was* the ideal length of an average par-4, and where should the tees be placed?

Marion consulted a variety of people and came up with what she believed would be a fair but testing standard. The measure would be the average length of three-time U.S. Champion Alexa Stirling's drives. Marion's own drives were not a good standard as her prodigious length was unattainable by all but a handful of golfers.

Alexa was asked to tee up over a variety of topography. The carry of her drives averaged 175 yards. Although this was then taken as a mean distance for placing hazards down the fairway, good design obviously required variations in the application. "Also on every hole," Marion wrote, "there are one or more alternate lines of play besides that of the direct line to the green. This permits the shorter or cannier player to attempt a safer line of direction, although usually it costs an extra stroke to do so."

This is an extraordinary statement, because it is an almost verbatim preview of the philosophy Alister MacKenzie will pronounce in his work for Marion a few years later at the Cypress Point Club and at Pasatiempo. It also describes perfectly Marion's own design of Cypress's legendary 16th hole.

At the Women's National Golf and Tennis Club, land was also allotted for tennis courts, stables, and a par 4 practice hole. At the lower end of the property was a fine old farmhouse. This was moved to the high ground and remodeled by the renowned architectural firm of McKim, Mead & White. More bedrooms were added, as well as a locker room, an office, card room, living rooms, and expanded dining area. From its location, there were only four holes which could not be seen from one of the verandas.

The first Board of Governors consisted of women well known in society and golfing circles. Marion Hollins was president; Mrs. Winthrop Aldrich, vice-president; Mrs. William Goadby Loew, treasurer; Miss Eleanor Mellon, secretary. Other board members were Mrs. Harold Pratt, Mrs. Childs Frick, Mrs. Thomas Hastings, Mrs. Howard F. Whitney, Mrs. Bruce Clark, Mrs.

Edward S. Knapp, Mrs. Monroe D. Robinson, and Miss Edith Cummings. Other early members included Mrs. Quentin Feitner, Miss Anita Lihme, Mrs. Joseph E. Davis, Mrs. Henry C. Phipps, Mrs. Norman K. Toerge, Mrs. Donald G. Geddes, and Mrs. G.M. Heckscher.

The club opened to great success, and it became a center of play for the champion women golfers of the day, as well as good and average golfers, wives of members of Meadow Brook, Piping Rock, the Creek and other nearby clubs; and Marion, of course, when she was east. On one visit she played an exhibition match with Gene Sarazen.

Commenting on the Women's National Golf and Tennis Club, *Golf Illustrated* credited "the tireless energy of the former champion for converting a dream of less than a year into a reality." *The American Golfer* in its coverage stated, "Because of the great variety of shots called for and in the wide choice of play open, the Women's National Golf and Tennis Club will greatly benefit the average woman's game. She will unconsciously become a better golfer [and] will find that certain shots are being executed that previously she had been reluctant to attempt."

Unfortunately, there is a terrible ending to the story. In 1941, just short of 20 years after the opening of the Women's National, with the Depression still in place, and World War II looming, Harvey Gibson, then president of the Creek Club, suggested that the two clubs merge. They were geographically very close, and a merger would effect economies in management and equipment. Each sex would retain their own course.

With some misgivings the women approved the merger. After all, many of them had husbands who were members of the Creek.* Marion, unwell in California, probably did not exert much influence in the discussion. Had she, perhaps the outcome would have been different. It was just 20 years earlier, after all, that the male exclusivity of most clubs had been one

---

* The Creek was a men-only club, as the following bears out: "To the members: With the Club in full operation, it is believed advisable to put into effect now the original plan of excluding Ladies from the Dormy House [clubhouse]. Therefore, until further notice, the entire Dormy House will be reserved for men. [signed] The House Committee, September 1, 1924."

The elegant clubhouse of the Women's National Golf and Tennis Club, designed by McKim, Mead, and White.

of the reasons for building the Women's National Golf and Tennis Club in the first place.

Gibson was head of the Manufacturer's Trust which held the mortgage on the Creek property. Under the terms of the mortgage the entire unpaid balance on the property was coming due. The governors of the Creek took the easy, but hardly honorable way out of their financial situation. Within a few months of the merger, they sold the entire property of the Women's National Golf and Tennis Club, and used the proceeds to pay off the mortgage.

That women were no longer banished from the Creek was a token that was beside the point, and many women never forgave their husbands the betrayal.

The former Women's National, modified and lengthened, is now the Glen Head Country Club.

Chapter Nine

Ernest Jones

Dedicated to the memory of my good friend, MISS MARION HOLLINS, founder of the Women's National Golf and Tennis Club

> —Ernest Jones's dedication of his very popular book, *Swinging into Golf*

Two of golf's most eminent instructors, Macdonald Smith and Ernest Jones, built all their teaching around the one conception, 'Swing the clubhead'...[and I know that] the one idea for the golfer to keep always in his mind is that, when playing a shot, his job is to swing the clubhead.

> —Bobby Jones in a testimonial to Ernest Jones

*I*n 1922 Marion Hollins was in England with the specific mission of locating a head professional for her new Women's National Golf and Tennis Club. She found Ernest Jones.

"I have talked to a good professional, one of the best on the other side, who will probably come to us as soon as we get started," Marion told *The American Golfer.* "This will be a wonderful opportunity for a girl to get the right kind of start, which is so important. On the other side they begin to play so very young, and get ahead of us by long experience, and I would like to see a great many young girls starting here with a good professional. Our club arrangements will make it possible for a girl to join the club alone, and to stay down there to play."

Ernest Jones was a scratch British golfer with a promising future professional career when he lost a leg in World War I. Back from the front, Jones returned to the golf course to find out whether or not he could continue with the sport. As he did not yet have a wooden replacement, he played his first round one-legged, dropping his crutches once he was over the ball. He shot a 38 on the outbound nine but, tired from walking the long course on crutches, he finished with an 83.

Jones's physical handicap required unusually fine balance. He also discovered a fundamental principle. "What you must realize is...that there is only one categorical imperative in golf, and that is: to hit the ball. There are no minor absolutes. There is only one thing you are allowed to hit the ball with, and that is the head of the club. So therefore the object is to use your power to transmit as much force as you are capable of producing into the clubhead."

From this Jones abstracted his simple maxim: "Swing the clubhead."

Once fitted with an artificial leg, Jones began breaking par on golf courses, but soon realized that his handicap better suited him to be a teaching, rather than a playing, professional. Because his instruction focused only on *swinging the clubhead,* other swing concepts his students had been exposed to disappeared.

That controls the clubhead? The hands, of course. Jones illustrated this with a primitive training aid: a penknife tied to the end of a kerchief. Swinging the knife worked nicely with the hands, a pure pendulum motion. The minute other body parts were consciously applied to increase the pendulum action, the bandana lost its straight-line tension, and/or the knife started making figure-eight patterns. The pure swing had a balanced rhythm, and Jones used to play waltzes which he believed provided a proper tempo.

Marion, herself, became known for humming the first bars of "The Merry Widow"—two beats on the back swing, two on the forward swing. She also introduced her family to a word which she felt described the moment at the top of the back swing. It was "poise," a word quoted later in a book about Ernest Jones's method. It is a wonderfully evocative word for the moment at which the backswing is smoothly converted to the beginning of the forward swing. Not pause, but poise.

Jones was convinced that the golf swing could be correctly performed only if it were conceived as one movement, under the control of the hands. If any other part of the body got into the action too soon, the swing was lost. It was Ernest Jones who went on from this observation to coin the now cliched dictum that the shoulders are "disastrous leaders, but wholly admirable followers." It was also Jones who, watching average instruction and play, came up with the oft-repeated maxim, "paralysis by analysis."

Some thought him controversial; his sole concern with the clubhead myopic. In the long run, however, Ernest Jones's reputation has survived. He is always on the short list of the top golf instructors of this country, and has been named one of the top three of the century by *Golf* magazine.

Installed in the Women's National Golf and Tennis Club, Ernest Jones began to work with the members who came for

Ernest Jones with his famous knife and kerchief training aid.

help in their game. The gamut ranged from novices and young players to national contenders. Under his tutelage, golfers who had struggled with their game began to win national championships. Over the years more than a dozen were won by his disciples, which included Helen Hicks, Henry Cotton, Leo Diegel, Virginia Van Wie, Betty Hicks, and Marion herself.

Few of Marion's golfing companions were still alive at the writing of this book, but two of them whom I interviewed, Betty Hicks and Virginia Van Wie (who died in 1997), remembered well their golfing days with Marion. In answer to the question about her contribution to the game of golf, they each included, "Swing the clubhead." Marion had sent them both to Jones, and each of them began to win national championships shortly thereafter, and kept on winning.

After the opening of Pasatiempo in 1929, Jones would divide his time, as the seasons dictated, between Marion's two creations, one on the West Coast, one on the East. Jones can be credited with more championships for his students than any other instructor in the history of golf, and it is estimated that he gave more lessons than any other teaching professional then or since.

To the end, when Jones ran his instruction out of an office in the old Spalding building in New York City, the penknife at the end of kerchief remained his training aid. Today, with high-tech video and an assortment of training devices, golf instruction has become very technical. The golf swing has been broken down into multiple components—a long way from the weight swinging on a string in a pendulum motion. As Bobby Jones (no relation) once said in a testimonial to Ernest Jones, the tendency in the P.G.A. is to take the golf swing apart, analyze the contribution of each body part in the motion, and then develop it step by step. "But we know perfectly well you can't teach it that way."

Virginia Van Wie, who won the National Championship three times before she retired from tournament golf, told me that before meeting Jones she had worked on her game in weight distribution, pivot, elbow in proper position at the top of the backswing, wrist cock as it should be, and still she could not win. At Marion's suggestion she went to Jones and immediately took the amateur trophy. Not only did her golf improve dramatically, she wrote, but she "learned that the game could be a joy and a pleasure instead of a mild form of torture."

In her 1932 Curtis Cup singles match, Van Wie was down three at the end of nine holes to Wanda Morgan, not an easy position from which to recover. She thought of Ernest Jones. "Here was a splendid opportunity to see if concentrating upon swing alone would prove itself sufficient. It is not always possible to swing, [as opposed to hit] but I know that to be the proper and best way to hit a golf ball, and by putting all my efforts [of] concentration on one thing, I discovered I stood a far better chance of succeeding in it. It worked, and I won 2 and 1.... [And, although I ignored all other elements,] professionals and good golfers have repeatedly told me how apparent these very fundamentals now are in my swing." Players and reporters alike, in commenting on the first Curtis Cup matches, remarked on the extraordinary grace of Van Wie's swing.

To this day, Betty Hicks, who gives a slide show lecture extolling the many pioneering roles of Marion Hollins, teaches the Jones method to students on a driving range in San Jose. Hicks was a nationally ranked player when she approached Jones at Marion's suggestion. After watching her hit a few balls, he commented: "You must have worked very hard to get as bad as this." Under his tutelage she went on to become U.S. Amateur champion and a pioneer of the L.P.G.A., placing high on the money list of the association in its formative years.

Jones' legacy today is not well known. In fact, although what he taught may be partially incorporated in a number of teaching philosophies, his name has largely slipped from currency. Manuel de la Torres teaches with Jones's philosophy in Milwaukee, and the Frankel Golf Academy at Jupiter/Hobe Sound in Florida is committed to a pure Ernest Jones methodology.

Perhaps a nice epitaph to Ernest Jones is this little poem, which he, along with Alister MacKenzie and Marion Hollins, used to recite and laugh over in California, as these three giants of American golf played their matches at Pasatiempo, and Jones lowered MacKenzie's handicap from double digits to below ten:

> The centipede was happy quite
> Until a toad in fun
> Said "Pray which leg goes over which?"
> This put his mind in such a pitch
> He lay distracted in a ditch
> Considering how to run.

Chapter Ten

Heading West

*I*n 1922 *Country Life* reported, "Miss Marion Hollins was the unfortunate victim of an illness last spring which seriously affected her sight. This was almost entirely responsible for her early and heavy defeat when defending her title gained in 1921, and everyone admired her pluck and sportsmanship in entering the event when so severely handicapped."

Marion went west to recover and did recover. At this time S.F.B. Morse was developing Pebble Beach and the Monterey Peninsula. He was impressed with Marion's energies, and hired her as "athletic director" of Pebble Beach. He also interested her in taking on real estate sales for the company.

One of the first things Marion did to promote Pebble Beach was to initiate annual golf tournaments for both men and women. Marion entered the inaugural event, which she won in 1922 and 1923. According to *The America Golfer,* "The great match of the 1924 tournament was that in which Miss Hollins defeated Miss Cummings, [the current national champion] 2 up. Miss Cummings took a two-hole lead early in the match and until the playing of the eighth hole looked a certain winner. On this hole, though, Miss Hollins threw caution to the winds and simply took the heart out of her opponent.... Miss Cummings elected to play safe and sent a mashie to the upper edge of the cliff. Miss Hollins took her brassie and smashed a screaming shot straight across the chasm to the green.... From then on it was all Miss Hollins."

The Pebble Beach tournament soon became the unofficial West Coast championship.

Even at the time when the Women's National Golf and Tennis Club was in its construction phase, and Marion Hollins was

*Marion Hollins sinking a putt on the 18th hole of the
Monterey Peninsula Country Club in the final match with
Mrs. Miriam Burns Horn, the national champion,
whom she defeated at the 20th hole.*

soliciting the membership, she was becoming something of a
commuter between the East and West Coasts. Very soon she
would be spending approximately half the year at each end of
the country, with cross-country dashes in between.

Back east in June of 1924 she won the Metropolitan Golf
Association championship finals 6 and 5, having been 7 up with
18 to play in terrific winds. The *New York Times* recorded the
event. (The *Times* and the *New York Herald* covered Marion's
activities, east and west, extensively during these decades.)
"Those who followed the match had the opportunity of seeing
Marion Hollins at almost the top of her form. Her amazing length
with her drive and brassie and the deadly accuracy with which

she played practically all her shorter shots were sources of per-
petual astonishment to the watchers.... In the qualifying round
her score was nine strokes lower than that of her nearest com-
petitor. She then marched through her opponents 8 and 7, 5
and 4, 6 and 5."

By 1924, however, Marion Hollins had become a West Coast
person. It was her home physically, and it also fit her personality. The west was still opening, exploring itself, challenging itself, a frontier without boundaries, the Pacific Ocean
notwithstanding. Marion would make fortunes in real estate
and oil. She was about to create two of the premier golf courses
of the world. She held records in golf and was winning important tournaments. She was playing polo with the men. She was
an excellent bridge player, and a very tough poker player. She
needed the open space and outlook of the west.

"She couldn't stand the East Coast after she once discovered California," her niece states. "She was just too big for ev-
erybody back east. Society women were not hiring engineers to
drill oil wells."

Though not beautiful, Marion had always been a good-look-
ing woman. The vigorous athletic life was more than sufficient
to keep her in good physical shape. She loved good food, however, and had the reputation of eating huge amounts. When
Marion moved west in 1922, she began to grow into hefty proportions. It was almost as though she physically expanded into
the new space she had discovered. According to her niece, she
simply didn't care about her appearance.

If the East Coast no longer fit Marion, we nonetheless find
her going back time and time again. She is frequently signing
her name in the guest books of the family places in the east.
Sometimes her mother or a brother writes, "Marion arrived
today...." And then there is her own entry, usually describing a
frenetic itinerary. Lake Placid, Buffalo, Virginia Hot Springs,
and the Equinox in Vermont, are some of her way stations.

> Arrived Christmas morning after a 600 mile trip
> Sunday. Have seen Aiken, Palm Beach and Miami now
> off for Charleston, Myrtle Beach with Ollie Iselin, then
> Middleburg Virginia, and on the 11th bound west.
> Will admit your grapefruit [South Carolina] are better
> than ours.

*Two champions of the links meet at Atlanta: Bobby Jones and
Marion Hollins, the National Woman's Champion in 1921,
who played in an exhibition foursome at the
East Lake Country Club in Atlanta.*

(On that trip she also stopped in Atlanta where Bobby Jones had organized an exhibition match with her, in her honor.) And,

"Marion arrives from Pebble Beach. Off to Paris on *Olympic.*" (She stops at Meadowfarm for six days upon return.) "Marion arriving September 10th on *Leviathan,* off for Hot Springs the 19th then to Pebble Beach."

Marion could not stand the east for very long, and the family was quite content that she came in short doses. One niece says that when Marion arrived the telephone never stopped ringing, and when she wasn't on the phone, her multitudinous interests and the energy with which she promoted them were exhausting. "She *was* exhausting."

Business, of course, brought Marion east. There were the specific missions to promote West Coast real estate and golf club memberships, and to fund her oil explorations and Pasatiempo. She was so effective in real estate that Samuel Morse underwrote the expenses of a New York City office which she opened in the old Heckscher Building at 277 Park Avenue. The walls of the office were covered with panoramic color photographs of Pebble Beach, the Monterey Peninsula, Carmel Valley, and later, Pasatiempo. Prospective buyers, drawn from her large acquaintanceship with wealthy New York society, could not help being dazzled by the stunning vistas they beheld.

But traveling east, Marion also came "home." "Home" was a geographic entity. It is where she grew up: where her father had introduced her to golf, and her mother to horses; where she had participated in decades of sports with brothers and friends. All these people still lived there for the most part. It was only she who had left home to find a new life.

Her childhood home would have provided something her new world could not: a sense of beginnings, of continuity. Meadowfarm would have been a haven of security and serenity. Her bedroom would still be hers, unchanged from one visit to the next. The dogs, the horses, her old pony would only gradually disappear from the scene, their offspring replacing them. It was a place where nothing changed.

In the world she created, Marion led a champion's life, complete with adoring friends, challenging projects, and, within

*Johnny Farrell, Glenna Collett, Marion Hollins, and
Walter Hagen after an exhibition match at
Pebble Beach. The women won.*

the sports world, recognition of her considerable accomplishments. It was not recognition she sought, however. As noted earlier it took a caddie to keep her focused. The trophies themselves she gave away to be melted down for the war effort. Later, according to her niece, she was just as likely to give some large silver cup won in a major tournament to a maid who had admired it while polishing it.

Perhaps, deep inside this ebullient person, there was a lonesomeness. With whom was she to share all her dreams, her triumphs? Marion Hollins never married, and the closest thing she had to a lifetime companion was her family.

Yet hers was most certainly not a solitary existence. Her high energy level generated a constant froth of social activity—house parties, impromptu steeplechase races, sunset picnics, trips here and there to visit friends. And in any function Marion was invariably the center of attraction. When Mary Pickford was going through her divorce from Douglas

Fairbanks, Marion took time off to move into Pickfair and manage the social calendar.

It is hard to imagine the day-to-day or week-to-week life of Marion Hollins. We are told of her boundless energies and enthusiasm for whatever she was involved with. Her notations in the family scrapbooks can be described as breathless: here today, gone tomorrow. With so many grand successes, some of them left for us to enjoy to this day, it would be nice to know what a period of a few weeks of Marion's life at this time might have looked like. There are two publications which give us a fragment of a view, just before and after her trip east to compete in the 1924 Metropolitan Golf Association and United States Amateur Championships. In September 1924, *Town & Country,* in its wrap-up of items of interest in society, took note of Marion. "Miss Marion Hollins, who has spent a large part of the year in California, was responsible for much that went on in the way of merry-making [at Pebble Beach], and the last effort of hers, before she concluded her sojourn has gone on record as an overwhelming success."

Staged by Marion at Del Monte, California, the merrymaking is described in the magazine as a one-week pageant of equestrian activities. Aside from the week of saddle events, gymkhanas, horse shows, and riding competitions, there were special events, normally done on foot, but in this case on horseback. Miss Nancy Heckscher, a well-known horsewoman from the east coast, won the egg and spoon race. There were musical chairs—or rather musical saddles. Marion herself won the mallet and ball race in the women's division, while Robert Hunter, Jr., who would help in the construction of the Cypress Point Club, won the men's counterpart.

Town & Country went on to note that Marion was off to Tahoe, then east where "she will also attend the international polo matches, renewing acquaintance with several of the famous poloists with whom she played in England and in this country."

At just this time back in Long Island, Dorothy McBurney, a childhood friend of Marion's, had suffered a number of throat and sinus problems, and had been told by her doctor to move to a better climate. As she lay bedridden, Marion arrived from the west: "The same old cheerful Marion of our childhood, and full of 'Prospects' as she called her real estate in Pebble Beach."

Marion Hollins at the 7th hole, Pebble Beach, Edith Cummings watching.

A wedding party at Marion's home in Pebble Beach. Her father; niece Evelina Hollins; her mother; niece Lilias Hollins, the bride; and her husband Reginald Frost; sister-in-law Lilias Hollins; Marion; her nephew Robert Hollins. Standing: her brothers McKim and Harry, Jr.

Marion visited her friend often, and suggested that she, her husband Mac and their young children all come to Pebble Beach. "I will get you a house and two Chinese servants," she persuaded.

And so they all boarded the train bound west, including Marion's brother, "blue-eyed Kim, full of charm but addicted to getting into hot water." (Kim, who had been given a job on Wall Street by his uncle, had had to leave after irregularities were discovered in some of the books. It was alleged that funds were missing and checks had been forged.) "He was going ostensibly to help Marion in her real estate business, but in reality to be chaperoned and looked after by Marion." [From *The World is so Full,* by Dorothy McBurney (Noyes).]

In some way Marion had become friends with a Mr. Harvey who had developed a chain of restaurants which serviced, among other things, railway depots. Dorothy McBurney recalls that at each stop they were presented with baskets of food: "fresh strawberries, asparagus, and delicious fresh pink trout," always "compliments of Mr. Harvey." When they weren't eating, they played bridge, and the loser of a rubber had to walk the dogs at the next train stop.

While entertaining the McBurneys, Marion was also preparing for the Pebble Beach championship tournament, "practicing diligently to keep her laurels and spending hours every morning perfecting this or that shot, sometimes with a professional to give her advice. But more often alone with a caddie to chase her balls," McBurney noted in her diary.

After she won the tournament, Marion took them on a trip through the Mohave Desert.

How was all of this possible? After all, this was not an idle time in Marion's life. She was selling Pebble Beach real estate, and managing the tournaments there; she was running a real estate office on Park Avenue; and she was busy putting together the membership of the Women's National Golf and Tennis Club, as well as overseeing the remodeling of its clubhouse and the construction of the course itself.

Chapter Eleven

Cypress Point, The Course

The 15th and 16th holes at Cypress Point.

WHEREAS, Marion Hollins has been granted by this corporation an option for the purpose of forming a golf club on properties of this company, under the laws of this state, to be known as the Cypress Point Golf Club, and,

WHEREAS, said option is still in force and effect, and said Marion Hollins has requested that a resolution and declaration in the form hereinafter set forth, be passed, authorized and executed by this corporation; there, be it

RESOLVED: That is the said Marion Hollins shall exercise the option aforesaid then and in that event this corporation will cause to be executed by its President and Secretary and under its corporate seal, a declaration in the following form to wit:....

So began what was to become perhaps the most beautiful and challenging course ever built. The records appear clear that, except for a period of a few months when she was immobilized with a bad back, it was Marion who was the driving force in the creation of both the course and the club's membership. In contemporaneous newspaper and magazine articles, she is called "the founder of the Cypress Point Club."

As to whose *idea* it was, there is some disagreement. Roger Lapham, one of the original organizers of the club, credits Marion. S.F.B. Morse, in a portion of his unpublished autobiography dictated in the 1960s, definitely points to himself: "I had conceived of the club and was responsible for its organiza-

*Marion Hollins standing on the planned site of the 1st green
at Cypress Point during the design phase. This photo
gives an idea of the amount of loam which was
required to complete the course.*

tion...." and goes on to say that he introduced the idea to Marion.
He contradicted himself, however, in what he wrote for publications at the time.

"No one but a poet should be allowed to write of the beau-
ties of the Cypress Point Club.... Visitors from all continents
have crossed continents to see it. And who has gone away without classing it with the most picturesque bits of coast in the
world? Due to the vision of Miss Marion Hollins, this point will
become the property of the most select country club in America."

And in the magazine *Game and Gossip* which Morse published, there is an announcement of the Cypress Point Club's beginning: "Rapidly, very rapidly, the nationally discussed and exclusive Cypress Point Club on the Monterey Peninsula is becoming a reality. The course, first conceived by Miss Marion Hollins, famed woman golfer, will very soon begin to take shape under the matchless engineering of Dr. Alister MacKenzie, dean of English golf architects."

Once Marion had the land under option, she had retained MacKenzie to complete the design for the course. Initially she and Morse had selected Seth Raynor, whom she knew well from his assistance at the Women's National Golf and Tennis Club. Unfortunately, Raynor died before plans were complete.

MacKenzie laid out the 18 holes, with Marion never more than a few footsteps away. Robert Hunter and his son, Robert Jr., important figures in golf architecture and construction in the first three decades of this century, were in charge of the actual construction.

As the site was primarily an area of sand dunes, a great deal of soil had to be brought in. 17-Mile Drive needed to be rerouted. An argument, resulting in a flurry of correspondence, arose between the Cypress Point Club principals and Morse over the routing of the 14th hole and the Drive.

Marion Hollins to S.F.B. Morse: "Dear Sam, At the meeting of the Cypress Point Club Golf Club today I was told to ask you to have the road staked along the 14th fairway so that Mr. MacKenzie can see it Sunday morning and report to Van [William C. Van Antwerp] on Monday. Will you please see that this is done? It might be a good idea to wire Charley Olmsted."* Morse then cables Olmsted.

Hunter then wrote Morse, "Partly to give you plenty of room for your road and to avoid annoyance there and partly to save soiling about 500 yards of sand dune, I shifted the routing of the 12th, 13th, 14th and 15th holes. To situate the 14th green where Mr. Stafford suggests means contouring the fairway for

---

* The Olmsted brothers were famous landscape architects in Boston. Among other work, they had laid out New York City's Central Park. Marion was also familiar with them through assignments they had completed for various members of the Vanderbilt family.

about 100 yards and making a huge fill for the green. It means also covering with soil a large area of the sand dunes."

Morse wrote Hunter, "I really believe that if we do not make that alteration and change that we are going to be bothered by it the rest of our lives. I am reasonably sure that it will result in the death of several people, for it will make a nasty mess in the middle of the golf links...."

Marion, however, believed that the changes obligated by the new road layout could "be made of distinct advantage for the Club," and so the matter was resolved. The extent of dunes on the proposed site of the course was considerable, and one of the heavy costs of the construction was in the large amount of loam which it was necessary to bring in. The photograph of Marion standing on the site of the first green gives an idea as to what was involved.

The 16th hole at Cypress Point is the most photographed of all holes on all courses. It lies on one of the most spectacular pieces of coastline in the world, certainly surpassing any other as a golfing venue. The massive unobstructed rollers of the Pacific Ocean surge into the cliffs, sending spray and spume into the air. Seabirds wheel above the maelstrom and, below, seals and sea otters can be seen in the roiling water strewn with kelp.

One stands on the tee and looks across the ocean to the point of land where the green is situated. In his original preliminary plans before he died, Seth Raynor had envisioned the green out on the point, and had routed the hole as a par 4. His successor, Alister MacKenzie concurred with the conservative dogleg approach, which required a carry of less than two hundred yards.

Marion had disagreed, however. She argued that it should be a par 3, directly across the ocean. She wanted the hole to be an heroic opportunity. The men had told her that it was an impossible drive, but she thought otherwise. To prove her point, she teed up a ball and with a brassie sent it on its way across the water. Where her ball landed is today the center of the green.*

---

* Alister MacKenzie in his autobiography corroborates this. "To give honor where it is due, I must say that, except for minor details in construction, I was in no way responsible for the hole. It was largely due to the vision of Miss Marion Hollins (the founder of Cypress Point). It was suggested to her by the late Seth Raynor that it was

The hole is 231 yards from the back tees, all carry. To be short and left a few yards places the ball in a bunker. To be short in any other way sends the ball into the Pacific. To be long also is to lose the ball into the ocean. If that happens, as 1940 Masters champion Jimmy Demaret pointed out ruefully, "There is no relief. The only place you can drop the ball over your shoulder is in Honolulu."

There is one other interesting detail in the layout of the Cypress Point Club. "Pebble has six great holes—all those that lie on the coastline," expressed two-time U.S. Open champion, Julius Boros. "Cypress has eighteen of them, whether they lie on the coast or not." This was disputed by Jimmy Demaret, who found the 18th hole weak. "The Cypress Point Club is the best seventeen-hole course in the world."

In fact, there was another plan for the 18th hole, not widely known today. It exists still in the original documents. On October 10, 1927 in the same month that discussions of the routing of the 14th hole were being resolved, S.F.B. Morse wrote. "It is likely that there may be some slight adjustment wanted at the 18th tee. After the 18th tee is definitely located and if it does not interfere materially with our road at that point, I have agreed to do what I can to meet with the viewpoint of the architect and club members in the slight adjustment in the area in that region."

And what was that "slight adjustment"? Well, to understand what was being considered, one has to be familiar with the Cypress Point Club. Behind the 18th, if you look out to sea, you will notice an upcropping of ledge about 50 yards out in the ocean. In the original plan, the tee was to be placed there, and Alister MacKenzie drew up an architectural rendering of a suspension bridge that carried out to the ledge. In the engineering blueprints, the ledge was leveled and loamed. We can only guess about who conceived this plan, but it is so typical of Marion's spirited belief that anything was possible, and consistent with her inventive solutions to so many things, one has

---

a pity the carry over the ocean was too long to enable a hole to be designed on this particular site. Miss Hollins said she did not think it was an impossible carry. She then teed up a ball and drove to the middle of the site for the suggested green."

The famous 16th hole at Cypress Point.

to suspect that she was at least involved, and perhaps was even the originator.

However, it did not take long to realize that, although the specifications for the bridge were rugged, the Pacific Ocean was not going to leave the structure long intact, let alone the turf of the tee on the ledge. It was also entirely possible that a member or two might be swept away if they attempted to use the tee in stormy weather. The plan was shelved, but the blueprints for the bridge and tee location still exist in the safe of the Cypress Point Club.

When Marion brought the great English golfer Enid Wilson to Cypress, the latter remarked, "I fell violently in love with the Cypress Point Club, but I was so furious because I was so besotted with the beauty of it that I just couldn't hit a golf ball." Since then, countless golfers and writers have given the ultimate accolades to the course, but few today probably are aware that the founder of the Cypress Point Club was a woman. Yet there she is, a photograph of her hanging in the men's locker room, dressed in a tweed jacket, discussing the layout with MacKenzie, Hunter, and former national champion, H.J. Wigham.

*Marion Hollins discussing the construction of Cypress Point
with Alister MacKenzie, H.J. Wigham, former
Amateur Champion, and Robert Hunter,
an associate of MacKenzie's.*

Chapter Twelve

Cypress Point,
The Club

*The Cypress Point Club is perhaps the most cel-
ebrated small acreage in the world. In its very different
way it is not less beautiful than Yosemite Valley. To
have seen, if only once, that joyous meeting of land and
water; and those trees, noble, fantastic and incredible,
is to be haunted by the memory of them forever. I
believe that those of us who are to have the privilege of
playing over this course will never care to play over any
other, forever."*

—Gouverneur Morris, charter
member

*Principal credit for the formation of the club belongs
to Marion Hollins.*

—Game and Gossip

*I*t is ironic that a woman should have taken on the responsibility—been given the responsibility—of creating a membership for the nascent Cypress Point Club. Many of the original list were men already collegial, being members of the San Francisco Golf and Country Club and Burlingame Club, or drawn from the social set in Santa Barbara. It is interesting to note that Samuel Morse stated that the names of members in these clubs were "submitted to Miss Hollins" for approval. Marion certainly knew them. She was playing golf and polo with them, and was, herself, one of the leaders of the Pebble Beach social set.

"The Pebble Beach colony are watching the organization of the new Cypress Point Club directed under the guidance of Miss Marion Hollins. The newest eastern members are Mr. and Mrs. Sidney Fish and Mr. and Mrs. William Burden." (From *Game and Gossip*.)

After working with attorneys to develop Articles of Incorporation and By-Laws, Marion enlisted Mrs. William Van Antwerp of Burlingame and Mrs. Peter Cooper Bryce of Santa Barbara to help enroll the early subscribers.

The land which Marion had optioned would be sold to the club for $1,000 an acre. "Miss Hollins estimated that the cost of constructing the links would be about $150,000, but to be on the safe side advised placing the figure at $200,000. The cost of constructing the club house was suggested at $100,000, but on second thought $150,000 was considered nearly right."

To finance this, the original plan was to have a membership of between 400 and 500, each member buying in at something just over $1,000. This strategy was revised when it became apparent that it would be easier to get "200 men or women" with an ability to subscribe for $2,500. The founders also realized that a good number of these members would be living elsewhere and, because the course could handle more play, they agreed that there should be a category of associate members with no voting rights who would pay modest dues. $100 was the suggested annual figure. This idea, unfortunately, was never activated.

Marion went to work with a flurry of handwritten letters to Lapham, Morse, and Morse's secretary, Miss Macdonald, about prospective members, fees, and the like. During this part of the work, she did not forget the construction. In one letter she chastens Morse: "The agreement is not ready.... It is most important that we have the meeting the first part of July.... Will you please tell Miss Macdonald to send out the notices not later than June 29th. Work cannot start until we take up the land and the only thing in the way now is the Agreement. It is *absolutely* important that the golf course be started inside of 3 weeks or we lose a year. I am counting on you to see that the agreement is ready this week. Cheerio, Marion."

The letters are written on letterheads from the Del Monte Lodge, Hotel St. Francis in San Francisco, and Del Monte Properties Company (at the Crocker Building, San Francisco). One is written by her brother Kim, enclosing two memberships and explaining that Marion is again laid up with her bad back.

A good salesperson is always looking for the moment "to close," that moment when the deal can be secured. As a promoter for the Cypress Point Club, Marion Hollins did not miss a beat. Just as soon as the figure of 200 members at $2,500 had been agreed upon, she wrote Roger Lapham, "I could do a lot to help by getting right on the job. At the end of three weeks we could form a pretty good idea of how things are going. Personally I do not think it necessary to have any other members of the committee present to decide how the Club should be formed, do you? It is so hard to get everyone present and *now that people are keen, let's jump on them.*" [Emphasis added.]

The membership grew initially to over 100, but in the depression years the number shrank, at one time to less than 50. S.F.B. Morse deserves the credit for saving the club from financial disaster. His company, Del Monte Properties, waived the interest due on the installment purchase of the property and for money loaned by Del Monte for the construction of the club-house. "I doubt," Morse recalled, "if there are any members of the club alive who know that this meant a loss to the Company of not far from $300,000.... Finally, with the very beneficent attitude of the Company, the club was able to discharge its debt entirely and is now in a very strong financial condition."

There is a photograph of Marion standing on the site of what will be the 16th tee with Grantland Rice, the great golf writer and editor. She is showing him the great beauty nature has provided and what she is building. Shortly after the photo was taken, Rice writes, "There is certainly no other location now known to the explorer or discoverer that so lends itself to every detail that makes up a golf battlefield of spectacular effort...there are only certain locations upon the earth which lend themselves to the making of an ideal links—where there is the seaside breeze and the seaside sand—where there are dunes and dips—knobs and valleys, and where in addition there is just enough foliage to soften any bleakness that may crowd upon the scene. There are many thousands of golf courses in the world, but only a few great ones. There is only a small cluster, to name such links and courses as the National, Pine Valley, Lido, Pebble Beach, El Cabellero, St. Andrews, Westward Ho, and a few others who take high rank.

"There are possibilities at the Cypress Point Club which surpass any of these named; physical possibilities that no other single golf domain can quite match."

What is ironic (and I find touching looking at that photograph of her) is that, because of the small membership in the club, few people have ever had the opportunity to marvel at this unique landscape about which she was so proud and ebullient. If at least the original plan for associate members had been implemented, many more serious and appreciative golfers would have visited Marion's Elysian Fields. A woman with a philosophy of inclusiveness well beyond her time, Marion surely would have found a solution to this limitation.

The creation of the Cypress Point Club would have been a crowning achievement for anyone. Marion, however, was yet to reach her summit. A fortune she would soon acquire would allow her to design and build a second course of supreme golfing terrain, her own "font of happiness," Pasatiempo, which is open today to public play.

*Marion Hollins, Mrs. Van Antwerp, and Grantland Rice
surveying the 16th hole layout at Cypress Point.*

But just as there are the ascents, so are there the descents.
In less than two decades she will die alone, down the road from
the Cypress Point Club, where the members played on, unaware.

Chapter Thirteen

Marion Hollins Strikes Oil in the Kettleman Hills

*D*uring the last years of the 1920s a number of significant things were going on in Marion Hollins's life more or less contemporaneously. Without an attempt to keep the chronology exact, let's begin with Marion's extraordinary acumen and belief that oil could be found in the Kettleman Hills.

William Marland, a California businessman, thought there might be oil in this desolate piece of land in the San Joaquin valley. He ran some shallow test drillings, but found nothing. He then withdrew from the venture, although the Marland Oil company continued to exist. Its president was Franklyn Kenny, a friend of Marion's in Pebble Beach. He believed that oil did exist. The government drilling permits were soon to expire, however. Typical of Marion, she began a crash study of the geology of the area, and became excited with the thought that Kenny was right.

Marion headed east where she had been selling one thing or another for a decade. First she went to Payne Whitney, an old family friend, and, with her bubbling confidence in this venture, she convinced him it was worth the speculation. More than that, she soon had him spreading his enthusiasm to others.

Before she returned west, she had secured participation from financiers Harold Talbott, Jr. and Samuel McRoberts; the industrialist Walter Phelps; a British businessman and personal friend Cecil Baker; as well as Walter Chrysler, the auto magnate. Her West Coast investors included John McGee and Sidney Fish, both of Pebble Beach. To handle the business she created a corporation in which the investors and her brother Kim and herself were the shareholders. It was called the

Kettleman Oil Corporation. The initial capital of $100,000 was used mainly to finance the government permits, Whitney having persuaded Ogden Mills to do the drilling for a share in the company. Mills brought in the Mexican Seaboard Oil Company rig, and drilling began.

Deeper and deeper they drilled, but there was no oil. Money was running out, and Marion returned to the east, anxious. Her belief, however, had not been shaken. They just needed to drill deeper, she told her family and investors. There was more drilling, but still no oil. Marion was getting desperate; everyone else wanted to abandon the speculation. She begged for a few more days of drilling.

On October 9, 1928, deeper than any drilling anywhere heretofore, the Kettleman Oil Corporation hit what it had been hoping for. An explosive force of oil and gas erupted from deep in the earth at a pressure of 5,000 pounds per square inch. It blew the drilling rig into the air, and a gigantic geyser of oil shot to the sky. Marion and her little band of believers had just tapped the richest oil field ever known. Once capped and tapped, this first well produced 100,000,000 cubic feet of gas and 4,000 barrels of oil daily.

Suddenly the Kettleman Oil Corporation was the darling of the industry with many suitors. In short order, Standard Oil Company of California and a partner bought out Marion and her fellow investors. Her share of the profit was $2,500,000, a tidy sum in the swirl of the Great Depression. Her brother urged her to place part of it into a trust for her protection, but she refused. She did establish a trust for the well-being of her parents in their later years, but to the newspapers she announced that the balance would all be invested in her Pasatiempo property.

A few years before this wealth of black gold erupted, three friends were drinking and having a good time in the old Monkeyshines Room (now the Tap Room) at Pebble Beach. After a final nightcap, they made a late-night lighthearted agreement: whichever of them was first to ever make $1,000,000 would hand over to each of the others $25,000. The trio were Marion; California's foremost polo player, Eric Pedley; and Louise Dudley, a nationally ranked tennis player. At the time, none of them had much money and while not exactly living hand-to-mouth, the trio were working at jobs to support their sports.

*The Kettleman drill blows as 5,000 lb/square inch
of soil and gas erupt.*

*Marion Hollins in a gunfighter's pose after striking oil
in the Kettleman Hills.*

Marion did not forget. At Pasatiempo she organized an elabo-
rate dinner party for 100. The tables were decorated with model
oil derricks and statues of galloping horses. The walls were lined
with garbage cans in honor of Louise Dudley who was then in
the waste removal business in Santa Monica.

Louis Butler, a prominent San Francisco attorney and friend
of Marion's, was master of ceremonies. As dinner neared the
end, he rose and delivered a speech. In it he went on and on
and on about Marion's oil find, and the fact that she was creating a trust in the amount of $25,000 for Pedley and Dudley. As
he laboriously went through the details of these trusts, the
hearts of the two awardees sank. They were as cash poor as
they had been the night of the wager at the Monkeyshines Room.
And then, Butler broke into a broad smile: the trusts were to
expire at midnight, two minutes hence. Marion, grinning, got
up and handed them each their checks. Just another one of
her elegant pranks.

Chapter Fourteen

Big Sur and Carmel Valley

The ground floor was constructed of patio rounds cut from local redwood trees 9 inches thick and squared to fit together checkerboard fashion and set in a sand cushion.... The lumber was split from local redwood logs using a sledge and wedges for the large pieces and a maul and froe to make thin boards. All wood materials were smoothed using the broad axe, adze, draw knife, and plane. The roof on the log cabin was constructed of shakes manufactured on the site, split by hand with a wood maul and shake froe.

—Roy Trotter, "Notes on Log House"

*M*arion was "cooking." She had cashed in on her oil speculation. She was winning golf tournaments on both coasts.
She had just competed in the Ladies' Amateur Championship
in St. Andrews. And, having bought the 570 acres above Santa
Cruz, she was moving Pasatiempo briskly along in its development phase (see Chapter 16). This did not stop her from taking
the train east to join her mother on the steamer for another
tour of France. There is a postcard from Tour d'Argent where
Marion had caviar and they ordered the restaurant's famous
pressed duck (ducks numbered 969, 970). There is a letter she
wrote to her niece on the back of a menu in Beaune, "where I
have been before...very French...very quiet this time of year...."

While all this was going on she somehow found time to take
Muriel Vanderbilt on a packhorse trip into Big Sur. There she
would buy 10,000 acres of the prime coast.

For those unfamiliar with it, Big Sur is one of nature's great
sculptures. The Santa Lucia mountains cascade down to a turbulent ocean far below. Today it is a popular spot for vacation-
ers and tourists precisely because of its picturesque splendor.
It is also the site of very expensive homes set high above the
Pacific.

Prior to the 1930s, however, there was no access by road,
and the mountains' deep canyons, which spread like fingers
to the sea, were impassable along the coast until a series of
bridges were constructed. What trickle of traffic did exist was
horse or mule borne, and relied on a trail high in the hills above
the canyons.

Big Sur had always been a wild, unsettled country. During
the time it was owned by Spain, and later under Mexican rule,

only a few land grants were issued in the area, and the Santa Lucia range cut off most exploration and commerce.

Before the arrival of the white man, Big Sur had been sparsely peopled by Essalen Indians, believed by ethnologists to be the first California tribe of native Americans to become extinct. Their numbers were always small, estimated to have been less than 1,000 at the time the Catholic missions arrived. Disease and forced labor at the hands of these missions eradicated the Essalens within a few decades.

After Big Sur became part of the United States, a few homesteaders straggled into the region and settled on the land which had been cleared by the Essalens. However, eking out a life on this coast was never easy, as livestock was vulnerable to the many mountain lions. Homesteaders shot game, grew vegetables, and planted orchards. The only commercial activity was taking the bark off oak trees, which was then shipped by water north to the tanneries. Even in the late 1920s, transportation of goods in and out by trail remained an arduous labor, and homesteading was dying out.

Into this remote landscape of pioneering subsistence rode Marion Hollins, for what original purpose we do not know. She would have taken the old coastal trail which ribboned its way along the high ground inland behind the canyons. This narrow track, worn by centuries of horse travel, had no formal right of way, but traversed homesteading property. Travelers were always welcomed in the small log homes, and Marion must have asked a lot of questions as she surveyed the magnificent country.

She learned the lay of the land, she learned of the hot springs which would soon bear her name, and she learned that many of the small holdings could be purchased, to create a large parcel of land. And so, like William Randolph Hearst who would follow suit at San Simeon abutting her to the south, Marion Hollins began to consolidate ownership of land. By the time she had finished, she owned from Rat Creek in the North to Limekiln Creek in the south, approximately eight miles of coast, ranging from one and a half to seven miles in depth back from the Pacific.

It was—and is—a stunning piece of real estate, and the breathtaking vistas were not lost on Marion. She soon had a plan for the property that was equally grand. She was going to

The view south from Marion's lodge at Big Sur.

create a splendid ranching retreat for her friends, especially the actors and actresses of the silent film era who had not made it into the "talkies."

There would be a central lodge and a series of cabins for the guests. The fishing and hunting possibilities were unlimited, as were the riding trails. A farm was also envisioned to round out the bucolic experience.

The grand plan never fully evolved, but considerable work was done. William Wurster (see Chapter 16) designed the lodge, which was built at an altitude of 1,200 feet with sweeping views up and down the coast. It was located near an established fruit orchard left by a former homesteader. The building still exists, today enclosed within the hermitage of the Camaldolese monks who now own the land.

Also completed was a road and bridge-building project deep into a canyon, of complex engineering design, to allow access to a hot spring, today known as Hollins Hot Springs. At the site, a cabin designed by William Wurster and complete with modern amenities was constructed. It was set in a narrow valley filled with giant redwood trees. The cabin burned some years ago, and only the chimney and the hot spring remain today.

When Marion's finances began to go sour she decided she had to sell part of the land. She approached John Nesbitt, a radio personality of the day. His widow recalls him telling Marion he had no interest in owning land in the remote wilderness. Marion was no ordinary salesperson, and "she began to work on him." Finally, exasperated, he asked her: "If I agree to go down with you to look at the land, do you promise you will never again bring up the subject?" She agreed, and of course he bought the land.

Throughout the 1920s Marion had been selling large parcels of land in Carmel Valley. Samuel Morse had acquired the land from the Pacific Improvement Company, and Marion brought Easterners out to see these "gentlemen's estates." Having no need of money at the time, she took her commissions in land. When she died she owned all the land that today comprises Carmel Valley Village, the airport, and the C.E. Holman ranch. Jimmy Wolter, whose family ranched the land for her, remembers her coming by, and how kind she was to him as a little boy.

Chapter Fifteen

The Curtis Cup

*To England in May, 1932, came Miss Marion Hollins,
with the pick of the Americans....*

—Enid Wilson

$\mathcal{F}$or decades amateur women golfers had sought a way to formalize an international competition between the United States and Britain. As early as 1913 the Curtis sisters from Boston had set up an informal international match to follow the U.S. Women's Amateur Championship of that year, held in Wilmington. The United States team consisted of Margaret and Harriet Curtis, Lillian Hyde, Marion Hollins (runner-up in the just completed Amateur), Nonna Barlow, Georgiana Bishop, and Katherine Harley. The British/Canadian team included Muriel Dodd, who won the 1913 British Championship and Gladys Ravenscroft, who had just beaten Marion in the U.S. Amateur Championship final. The British won the international tourney 5 to 4.

There continued to be informal matches over the years. In 1925, *Golf Illustrated* reported: "Although the project of a feminine edition of the Walker Cup has fallen through from an anticipated lack of funds and a lukewarmness on the part of the U.S.G.A. a great deal of interest is being shown in the international match which will probably take place in May. The proposed venue is Troon, on the West coast of Scotland, and the players who have expressed their willingness to make the trip are Miss Edith Cummings, Miss Marion Hollins and Mrs. Clarence Vanderbeck...."

As the idea gained currency at the end of the decade, some in Britain grumbled that a regularly scheduled international competition for ladies might begin to smack of professional athletics. When the formalization of the Curtis Cup matches was announced, Sir Ernest Holderness, former men's amateur champion, put his opinion quite bluntly: "No one could expect a married woman with growing children to win championships. That is a shocking thought. It would be enough ground for divorce."

As the late British commentator Peter Dobereiner wrote, "The British do not appreciate change, especially for the ladies. Golf has been soaking in the male chauvinist piggery for 500 years and so it cannot be eradicated overnight."

In 1932, however, it was finally going to happen: the initiation of a biennial formal competition between teams of the best amateur female golfers of United States and Britain/Ireland. It was christened "The Curtis Cup" in honor of the Curtis sisters who had so long sought such an event, and who donated the trophy.

Marion Hollins was to captain this first United States team. The event was to be played at Wentworth, England. Having allowed golf to play a secondary role in the years prior to the match due to her promotional work for Pasatiempo, Marion, as captain, would only be a reserve player along with Dorothy Higbee. The team was composed of Opal Hill, Virginia Van Wie, Helen Hicks, Glenna Collett, Maureen Orcutt, and Leona Pressler Cheney.

"I think we have a good chance," Marion told an interviewer. "In former matches, which have all been of a very informal nature, we have not had a representative team. The one which Glenna captained last year was the best so far, but it had its weak spots. The match ended with 8 games for the British to 6 for the Americans, and our girls were in difficulty from the very start since they went almost directly from the boat to the golf course."

Marion was going to handle her team very, very differently. They were going to go over early, and they were going to accustom themselves to the tournament course and format.

It almost did not work out as planned, however, as Virginia Van Wie (whose play at Wentworth would turn out to be critical) was not aboard the ship at sailing time. With great apprehension Marion searched the pier for her missing player. Visitors aboard the ship to see friends off were ordered to disembark. It was now three minutes to sailing time, and there was still no sign of her.

At this moment, Lincoln Werden of the *New York Times* was driving Virginia Van Wie at high speed through the New York City streets to the pier.

Virginia Van Wie had spent the previous days practicing at the Women's National Golf and Tennis Club and, after a final round on the day of sailing, was having lunch at Helen Hicks' home. Then it was time to leave for the ship. "I've forgotten my most treasured golf shoes at the club," she suddenly exclaimed in alarm. Werden drove her back to Glen Head to retrieve them, and then began the 1¼ hour drive to New York 1¼ hours before sailing time.

It was that time now. No Virginia Van Wie, and the crew had begun taking in gangplanks and singling up lines. Then, just as the last companionway was about to be hoisted by a crane, the car careened up to it, and Virginia Van Wie, with her luggage, clubs, and her precious shoes, boarded.

One slight disadvantage noted by advance press coverage was that the British players were considered longer off the tee. Marion felt that most of her team could average 220–250 yards, but more importantly, that "any woman good enough to be selected to represent America on the international team should be able to adjust her game to suit any condition." Because wind can be a significant factor on the British courses, Marion had asked the team members to prepare for the competition before they left America by playing different courses in windy conditions.

"She was wonderful in every way," said the late Virginia Van Wie, "and a great captain, great. And as a person. You know she brought her Irish maid from Pasatiempo over on the ship so that during the match she could go back to the town she had emigrated from."

The American team arrived in England by steamer a full week before the match. They settled into Great Fosters Hotel at Wentworth and, "to the mild astonishment of the locals," were to be seen practicing foursomes morning and afternoon, round after round on the tournament course.

What was going on? United States players were, and largely still are, unused to the foursome format in tournaments, in which two players hit alternate shots off one ball against a similar pair. That was to be the form of play for the first series of Curtis Cup matches, and Marion wanted to establish who paired best with whom.

Late in the afternoon on the day just prior to the Curtis Cup match, the British team arrived "in time for tea."

The U.S. Curtis Cup team being met by Joyce Wethered, British captain, at Waterloo Station, London. Left to right: Glenna Collett Vare, Dorothy Higbee, Virginia Van Wie, Opal Hill, Joyce Wethered, Marion Hollins (U.S. captain), Helen Hicks, Leona Pressler Cheney, and Maureen Orcutt.

On the morning of the first official international competition, the two teams assembled at Wentworth's east course. Recalled Virginia Van Wie, "There is no nervous strain in golf equal to playing an International Match. The true champion, however, regardless of whether her nervousness is apparent or otherwise, plays better golf under a strain. It rather keys one up for the battle. No one who rode to the Wentworth Club with the American team...would say a championship golfer has no nerves. Nervousness is shown in various ways, depending on the temperament of the person. I do not know how many girls noticed this fact during that short ride, but it was most apparent to me. Some were talking incessantly, others not saying a word, the majority of us yawning, a true sign of nervousness."

The nervousness and the week of practice served them well. "The competition began, and the home crowd was silenced. The unthinkable was happening. America won all three four-somes.... As the porters packed the American bags, the Curtis sisters took special care of their Cup which had taken a generation to give away. The trouble was that no one had the sense to recognize the fact that the Americans may have taken the cup, but they had left behind a free lesson in preparation." From *The Story of Ladies' Golf* by Malcolm Crane.

The largest crowd ever to follow a female tournament in England began with all the positive encouragement, then turned silent and, according to Maureen Orcutt, in the afternoon singles matches became unruly. The final score was United States 5½, Britain 3½. At its conclusion Joyce Wethered stated ruefully, "As events were to prove, Marion Hollins certainly made the wiser choice." And British team-mate Enid Wilson opined, "Downright shameful. We were left alone to do what we wanted. If you did not want to practice, you did not have to."

The U.S. team returned home aboard a French liner on which Marion happened to know, from prior crossings, the maitre d' of the premier restaurant. Virginia Van Wie recalls that this connection provided the team, already jubilant, with a luxurious crossing.

Chapter Sixteen

Pasatiempo

...an even more important part in this amazing development has been that played by the genial president of the organization, one whose name is internationally heralded in sporting circles and whose fame as a host, par excellence, has spread the length and breadth of a Commonwealth famous for gracious hospitality, California. It is under the directing genius of this "great character" as Marion Hollins is called by all who know her, that Pasatiempo has won its dominant "place in the sun" as the Western Riviera as well as the relaxation resort of many of Hollywood's most famous and glamorous stars.

—California Outdoors and In

Jean Harlow attended opening day of Pasatiempo's steeple chase season in 1931, as did other famous actors, authors, and society darlings. The champagne began to flow at Pasatiempo, and celebrities were always on hand to sip from the glass: Alice Marble, Will Rogers, Joan Fontaine, Mary Pickford, Claudette Colbert, the Rothchilds, the Vanderbilts, and Babe Zaharias. This was Marion's circle, and she shared close friendships with many. As a renowned golfer, she was able to break the barriers of the era's class system, which drew distinct lines separating the socially elite, sports figures, and entertainers.

—Rhonda Glenn

*T*he original image of what is today Pasatiempo is of such startling magnitude it hardly seems possible to have been the vision of a single person. But that was Marion. She funneled all her energy, enthusiasm, sporting acumen, and taste, into the development of what she conceived as the greatest golf course and sporting/residential complex in the country.

It was the culmination of everything that came before. Jerry Vroom in his history of Pasatiempo entitled it "The Elegant Dream." It is a perfect title. Where else in the 1920s was someone sitting astride a horse, envisioning a planned community of attractive houses surrounding a golf/tennis/equestrian/bathing facility?

However, this was not just a dream. Marion was accustomed to translating dreams into accomplishments. First she needed to purchase the rolling land above Santa Cruz which she had seen, surveyed on horseback, and already planned in her mind.

She headed east, following the same trail she had blazed to finance her as-yet-unsuccessful oil-drilling venture. She created the Santa Cruz Development Company as a financial vehicle and approached a family friend, F. Cecil Baker, an expatriate British financier and businessman. He fell prey to Marion's enthusiasm, and she had part of her money. Baker was wealthy, and owned a fine New York City penthouse with porches which contained his considerable vegetable garden and a most prized field of corn. Later, he would build his own house at Pasatiempo.

The 570 acres that Marion Hollins purchased with Baker's money had its own history. Fossilized sharks' teeth from a prehistoric time have been discovered in a barranca, grizzly bears once roamed this land, and more recently it was the camping ground of Ohlone Indians who harvested acorns from the large oaks. Early in the nineteenth century, the land became part of a tract that had been deeded by a Mexican land grant to an English soldier of fortune, William Buckle. He named the place Ranch Carbonero for the charcoal which the property produced from its oak trees. Buckle and his brother were rumored to have buried treasure from their privateering days near their adobe house on the high ground of what is today the 16th fairway. After their tenure, the land passed into other hands, but the gold was never found, or at least reported.

Marion, however, was not looking to the past. She was planning for the future, moving toward her dream, as always, with consummate energy. In fact, it took less than two years to go from her idea to opening day on the golf course.

Marion contracted the Olmsted brothers to create an overall plan that met her specifications for the golf course and its buildings, residential areas (which included in addition to houses, a hotel, elementary school, and shopping area), space for tennis courts, race track and polo field, as well as six miles of bridle paths and nine miles of roads.

Marion then retained Alister MacKenzie as architect for the golf course. History does not record how much design work Marion did herself on the Pasatiempo course. We know, however, that she had a stated philosophy of golf course architecture, that she had been directly involved in the design of the Women's National Golf and Tennis Club, and had been responsible for the layout and routing of least one hole at Cypress Point. Marion was on the scene during the actual shaping of the course, and no tree could be removed from the land without her permission.

There is one piece of evidence on the significance of Marion's architectural role in golf course design. David Owen is writing a book about the early history of Augusta National. In the course of researching the subject he has found a letter from MacKenzie, who had been requested to come to Augusta as the course was in the preliminary construction phase. MacKenzie wrote from Pasatiempo that he was unable to make the trip at the time but that he was sending his "associate, Marion Hollins." It is a remarkable statement.

Marion had always loved the links courses of Scotland, England and Ireland. Although the Pasatiempo land lay some dis-

*Opening day match at Pasatiempo. Cyril Tolley (British
Amateur Champion), Marion Hollins,
Bobby Jones, Glenna Collett.*

tance from the ocean, she managed to achieve some of the char-
acteristics of the links—hard fairways and deep bunkers.

While work was progressing, Marion went in search of an
architect who could design the graceful houses she envisioned.
She sent out requests for submissions of a model style. Marion
chose William Wurster's design, and what was to become known
as the "California ranch style house" was born. Wurster then
went on to a long and internationally acclaimed career.

"I was absolutely without a dime when Marion accepted my
design," Wurster recalled later. In a four-page single-spaced
letter he typed to her while she was back at East Islip, he wrote
that a phone call from her there "was my first time at that
distance." And, visiting the site of her home-in-construction,
he added, "Swimming Pool: Had my first swim on Wednesday
and found it darned pleasant."

Then there was the landscaping. Thomas Dolliver Church
had found little work when Marion took him under her wing.

She wanted extensive plantings, and she gave Church free rein in the landscaping of the residential properties. Collaborating with Wurster, Church created courtyard gardens which led into roofed-over spaces, appropriate to Pasatiempo's climate. In his two years of work at Pasatiempo these "outdoor rooms," especially, established his reputation. In his career, Church designed more than 2,000 gardens in the United States and Canada, and is considered the finest landscape architect of his generation.

It was Pasatiempo, not the lodge overlooking the Pacific in Big Sur, that became for a decade a retreat for the Hollywood crowd. The great golfers of the day were there as well, as were the polo set which included Spencer and Louise Tracy.

Added to this socially mixed group came East Coast society and the pillars of San Francisco and Burlingame social life. At a time when these diverse groups did not ordinarily mix, Marion tossed them all together into one large happy salad.

The opening day of the Pasatiempo golf course brought a crowd of more than 3,000 onlookers to watch an exhibition match between Marion, paired with Bobby Jones,* against three-time National Champion Glenna Collett and British Amateur champion, Cyril Tolley. From that moment on, for the next decade, golf was the club's center of activity. (Although if not golfing, Marion could often be seen from the course taking one of her horses over improvised hurdles.)

Marion's endless stream of houseguests could be found on the course at all hours. Friends, relatives, and ranking golfers played on what was soon known as the sportiest, and most difficult, test of the sport on the West Coast.

---

* That Bobby Jones selected Alister MacKenzie to design Augusta National likely stems from these days in California. Jones was familiar with the work of Donald Ross in the East, and also that of Charles Blair Macdonald and his associates. He would have played on some of the courses in this country that the British architects Colt and Allison had designed. He may have read MacKenzie's book on the architectural design of courses. Here, now, he was playing golf on one of his finest, Pasatiempo. He also played Cypress Point, and with Mairon bubbling her enthusiasm alongside, we can presume that it is the reason that MacKenzie found himself the architect of Augusta National two years later.

Marion Hollins' opening drive at Pasatiempo's opening day.

When the U.S. Women's Amateur was held at the Los Angeles Country Club in 1930, Marion invited the contestants for an extended golfing party at Pasatiempo. Helen Hicks, Maureen Orcutt, Edith Quier, Glenna Collett, Dorothy Campbell Hurd, and Virginia Van Wie, the champion women of the day, they all came. As always, Marion was the gracious host, sparing no expense in making a grand event, with prizes awarded for every conceivable performance.

In its heyday, Pasatiempo was a rich experience if you were a part of Marion's orbit, and it certainly was an eclectic group of characters that came and went.

- Harold Nicholson and Vita Sackville-West sign into the guest book at "Sleepy Hollow," Marion's home, for a few days. Why are they there?
- One day, Marion's Irish maid, Morgan, answers the front door. A woman is standing there with a golf bag.

Marion Hollins and Babe Didrickson Zaharias at Pasatiempo.

"Yes, Ma'am?" "Tell Miss Hollins da babe is here."
The maid dutifully trips on down to the living room.
"Miss Hollins," she announces, "Da babe is here."
Didrickson, new to golf, becomes a repeat visitor and
houseguest.

- Samuel Morse comes up from Pebble Beach to see
  how Marion is doing. It is drawing near the cocktail
  hour, and the two of them have a drink or two. She
  tells Morse that they have to behave because Lucrezia
  Bori, the great New York Metropolitan Opera diva, is
  due. The soprano does not show up on time, and
  Marion and Morse debate whether they can have another cocktail in the interim. Finally, there is a bang
  on the front door. Marion goes down the hall, Morse a
  few steps behind. She opens the door, and there is
  Lucrezia shrieking a greeting as she weaves around
  the porch, dead drunk.
- Joyce Wethered comes for an exhibition match.
- Mary Pickford is almost a fixture at Pasatiempo. At
  one point she and Marion fly to New York on a busi-

*Marion Hollins and Joyce Wethered after an
exhibition match at Pasatiempo.*

ness trip, the purpose of which is lost in time. They
stay at the Sherry Netherlands. Late for a meeting
one morning, Marion strode into the hotel, pushing
open the door with the vigor of her polo swing. At that
moment, the heavyweight boxing champion of the
world, Jack Dempsey, was heading in the opposite
direction. Dempsey, hit in the forehead by the edge of
the door, dropped unconscious to the carpet—a story
Marion loved to recount.

In those days, people in entertainment were not asked home
to dinner, though maybe they might be invited *after* dinner—to

entertain. But Marion wanted very much for Mary Pickford to see Meadowfarm and meet her family.

"She's in movies," was her mother's response. "Certainly not."

Marion brought her friend out to the family place, anyway. Her parents' maid, Pauline, was obsessed with movie stars, and spent her free time reading all the pulp Hollywood magazines. She was drying dishes in the pantry with her back to the door as they walked in. "Hello, Pauline. I want you to meet Mary Pickford." (It is hard to imagine the extent of Mary Pickford's popularity. When she and Marion walked into Grand Central Station, a stampede developed, and they were almost crushed by the fans of "America's Sweetheart".)

Under the graceful exterior spiral staircase in the back of Marion's house at Pasatiempo was a recessed porch fronted by lawn and framed by eastern wisteria, the classic Wurster/Church outdoor living room. This area, filled with chairs, tables, and large umbrellas, was known as "the cave." It was the epicenter of Pasatiempo's social doings. There were lunches, teas, late night carousing, early champagne breakfasts. Yet all the partying—and the bellows in Marion's hands never quieted—was not permitted to interfere with the sporting opportunities. Marion's houseguests and the hand-selected neighbors were almost all amateur athletes of the first caliber.

It wasn't just ordinary golf, tennis, and polo, however. Marion loved pranks. In one 18-hole match against her niece, who was a scratch golfer, and her niece's husband, Marion played every one of her shots on one foot. And won. One loony game which she devised was donkey baseball. This required the batter to proceed to first base on a donkey after a hit. As the beast's sense of urgency to get anywhere, let alone down the baseline, usually was somewhat less than that of its burden, this made for some riotous wrangling over speed and direction.

In addition to the stream of guests, Marion assumed the role of looking out for "problem" members of the family. Her niece, Evelina, very beautiful and a fine golfer, was emotionally unbalanced. On one of her trips east, Marion took Evie in tow and brought her to California via a Grace Line steamer which stopped on the way in Cuba, Venezuela, and Panama. A wonderful trip, the niece recalls. Meantime, another niece, Phyllis, was already in residence, having been shipped out by Marion's

Will Rogers at Pasatiempo.

brother Gerald. Phyllis wanted to be a professional golfer, and although diminutive, was playing scratch golf.

Then there was her brother, McKim, universally known as Kim. Everyone remembers how charming he was, or was supposed to have been, and there are many amusing anecdotes about him. When he was at Harvard, playing on the golf team, he was invited down for the annual tournament at the National Links in Southampton, Long Island. He was paired against Oswald Kirby, a fine amateur, who went to bed early to prepare for the match. Kim, on the contrary, made a night of it, and by the time it was getting close to tee time had so overindulged he had forgotten where he was staying. Undeterred, he arrived at the course in tuxedo and pumps. Kirby, who was serious about the match, was not pleased. He became even less amused when

Kim found his dancing pumps too slippery on the grass, and played the rest of the daunting course in his stockings, winning 2 and 1.

On the west coast Kim was the attractive drunk, always welcome on the links for his graceful game, and at parties for his good looks and sense of humor. He lived in Marion's house at Pasatiempo until, on a bet, he married Ysabel Chase. She was a niece of the renowned Palm Beach architect, Addison Mizner, who designed a large house for them overlooking Cypress Point. Kim always needed more money than there was at hand, however.

One weekend a car full of houseguests, up from Monterey, pulled into Pasatiempo. "We could have sworn we saw Kim in a chain gang on the Watsonville Road," one of them told Marion. They were not mistaken. Kim was in trouble again.

As this is not a book about Kim, we will close him out at Marion's funeral. He arrived briefly at the church—some say he was intoxicated—and stated that it was too sad for him to stay, and that he would meet everyone back at Marion's place afterward. When the family arrived, Kim was not there. Nor were Marion's golf clubs, silver, and linen.

Although the rest of America was under the cloud of the Great Depression, at Pasatiempo these were the halcyon days, and Marion's guest book is filled with appreciations. "An experience in life I shall not forget." "The most real person I have had the pleasure of knowing." "A lovely lady who gave us a wonderful vacation." "A whirlwind of charm." The guests came from everywhere: New York, Bulgaria, St. Louis, Burlingame, St. Andrews.

Marion refused to listen to cautionary advice from her bookkeeper. The profits from her oil venture seemed to her inexhaustible, and in the prosecution of her dream there was a continuing agenda of new construction and new purchases.

Shortly after the golf course opened, Marion purchased a tract of prime ranchland in Scott's Valley, a few miles up the San Jose road from Pasatiempo. Her plan was to build a racetrack and stables for her horses. For the latter she turned again to William Wurster, who proceeded to design a dwelling for animals equal to what he created for humans. The horses were to have the best, his client had specified. Large box stalls were ventilated by chutes which were connected to a tower which

The 16th green at Pasatiempo in 1930. Marion is putting. Glenna Collett and Mrs. Dorothy Campbell Hurd are looking on.

The 18th green at Pasatiempo in 1930. The tee is in the distance, beyond the barranca. Marion scored a hole-in-one on this green.

brought in and circulated fresh air. On one side of the quad-rangle were the grooms' quarters and tack room. In addition there were bedrooms, bathrooms, a laundry, a kitchen, and din-ing room. The racetrack itself was never completed.

Simultaneously, Marion purchased a large portion of what today is the Small Craft Harbor of Santa Cruz, as well as sev-eral hundred feet of oceanfront beach. A Beach Club was formed for members of Pasatiempo, complete with clubhouse.

Marion Hollins was an excellent tennis player, as were many of her friends, including Eleanora Sears and Helen Wills, both national champions. So...tennis courts. They were built with the finest clay, imported from France. During the 1930s Helen Wills practiced at Pasatiempo before major tournaments, and also frequently played exhibition matches there.

Pasatiempo was now purring along with its golf and tennis events, and Marion was moving on with new ideas and plans. In June of 1930, she was instrumental in the formation of the Pacific Coast Steeplechase and Racing Association with a cir-cuit of racing in northern California. The Association's first vice presidents included Marion Hollins and Samuel Morse.

In 1931 the first steeplechase meet was held at Del Monte, where 4,000 spectators lined the track. Two weeks later the meet was at Marion's track at Pasatiempo. This was a momen-tous occasion for the city of Santa Cruz. A special train was organized to bring horses, grooms, special guests, and automo-biles into Santa Cruz, and more than 7,500 spectators showed up for the seven-race schedule. A hunt ball was held the night before the meet for the owners, which included New York stables as well as West Coast entrants and their guests, followed the next day with a lunch for 100 at Marion's house prior to the races. It was all a huge success.

The City Council of Santa Cruz adopted a resolution of ap-preciation for all her work in bringing this major event to the area. The *Santa Cruz Sentinel* reported, "Starting in an elabo-rate way with the golf course, Miss Marion Hollins increased her program until today she has the showpiece of the west, not even equaled by the old established Del Monte course or other holdings of Morse." On the following year, the crowd in atten-dance almost doubled, and a local newspaper reported that "Pasatiempo became the steeplechase center of the Pacific coast." As usual, Marion had built the finest, the sandy soil

Steeplechase Course at the Pasatiempo Country Club, Santa Cruz.
A part of the golf course shown in the background.

supporting a fine turf which made the track similar to the great English venues.

And then there was polo. A California newspaper cited a quote from the 1930s: "What Babe Ruth was to baseball, Marion Hollins was to polo." It is hyperbolic, but at least it is an historical counterbalance to today's ignorance of Marion Hollins as not only dominant in women's polo, but unique in her frequent matches with the leading male players of the world.

Women's polo hardly existed in the west in the 1920s. Marion played polo at Del Monte with the men's teams, often including her pal Eric Pedley, then a 9-goal player. One day, after Marion had moved to Santa Cruz and Pasatiempo was in full swing, she and her friend Dorothy Demming Wheeler went to the races. Wheeler wanted to place a bet on number 9. Marion went to get the tickets, but absentmindedly bought number 7. She became embarrassed when an old tout opined, "Dat numba seven hoss shore am lame. Ah bet she can't roun' de track let lone win dat money for you, Miss Hollins."

Number 7 was in fact a bit lame, but number 7 won the race, paying $450 to the dollar. With her winnings, Dorothy Demming Wheeler built a small polo field in Santa Cruz.

With long-hitting Marion Hollins playing at back, Wheeler and two others had a polo team which went out and won some tournaments. They also began to play the men's teams.

Marion, of course, had to have a polo field at Pasatiempo, and one was built. She also fielded a team, and there were frequent weekend matches. Polo was becoming popular in Hollywood, and it is not surprising that Walt Disney and Spencer Tracy, who both played, journeyed up to Pasatiempo. Tracy's wife, Louise, even deserted home ground and joined Marion's team, which beat Riviera in the inaugural Governor's Cup competition.

1936 and the first 11 months of 1937 were grand times for Marion. At Pasatiempo, the high level of activity accelerated. The new swimming pool opened with a gala reception. Mary Pickford and Buddy Rogers, Brian Aherne and other movie stars flew up in a private plane, and old friends from the east were on hand. Marion played an exhibition golf match with professional trick-shot specialist Joe Kirkwood, who thrilled the audience by going the complete round using only a broom handle and a shovel.

*The Pasatiempo polo team after winning the Governor's Trophy
by defeating Riviera in the final game.*

*Louise Tracy (wife of Spencer Tracy) and Marion Hollins
just off the polo field.*

Marion traveled down to Los Angeles for Mary Pickford's and Buddy Rogers's wedding. A quick note to Mildred Yorba MacArthur, a star in California amateur golf, indicates Marion's continued level of enthusiasm. "I will be at Mary's again Saturday night, and will probably remain two or three days, so I will bring my golf clubs, and perhaps we can arrange to have a match. I will be busy on Sunday, as I promised to play a few chukkers of polo, and have been so busy all summer that I haven't had time to do any playing, so want awfully to do that."

These were happy times—for her loyal friends and for those who came to sponge. Where else during these years of widespread financial crisis were stables being erected, polo fields and teams established, and some of the country's finest golf holes being played after champagne breakfasts?

Marion never tired of taking one and all out for a round of golf, and was often part of a locally famous foursome of the early 1930s: Marion and Ernest Jones (who spent his winter months at Pasatiempo while the Women's National was closed) against club professional Adrian Wilson and Alister MacKenzie. On one of the matches the latter pair had won 2 and 1 on the 17th hole. "We'll finish it out just to prove you were lucky to win," said Marion with her cheerful smile. She teed up her ball on the 18th and took out a four-iron. She sent the ball flying over the barranca and dead into the hole. It was Marion's fifth hole-in-one, having scored her fourth at Cypress Point a few months earlier.

Marion held a "tee party" in honor of Alice Rutherford and Charlotte Glutting, two rising East Coast stars. Attending were most of the top female players of the west. In the afternoon Marion and Babe Didrickson played an exhibition match against the champion and runner-up in the Pasatiempo Club's men's division. The women won as Marion on that day "could not miss a 20-foot putt." As the match progressed the female gallery began giving the men a good roast for being bested by two women. A tournament for all the assembled women then took place. The occasion was so successful that Marion was asked to make it an annual event.

Little did anyone realize that the money was running out. It was not a time to be buying vacation houses and her real estate prospects were few. The Pasatiempo clubhouse was serving few meals, and getting even fewer greens fees. Marion's accountant told her she was spending $5,000 a week on the Pasatiempo staff of more than 30, in addition to new capital expenditures. But she did not take note.

She headed for the Northern California Golf Tournament, which she won, sending news of the victory to her parents by telegram at 6:49 A.M. Commenting on the tournament, Scott Chisholm, widely read for his "Bletherings o' Boles McCracken," wrote, "Miss Marion Hollins, recently christened by this writer 'The lass o' Pasatiempo' because she owns and operates the bonnie Pasatiempo Country Club at Santa Cruz, walked away with the Northern California Women's Championship last month.... That made all present very happy, even her victim, because Marion is the darlin' o' the gods so far as sportsmanship an' charm o' person are concerned."

Then there were all the matches she was called over to Pebble Beach for. High profile visitors frequently came to Pebble with the thought of buying land and settling. Naturally, there were good golfers in the mix, as the links were one of the attractions. Samuel Morse used to enjoy setting them up for a big stake match in a mixed foursome, where the "home team" was championship golfer Jack Neville who had designed the course, and Marion.

By early 1937 Marion was in financial trouble. What had seemed an inexhaustible reserve of wealth was depleted. She had never learned how to cut back, and had continued to pay the airfares for indigent relatives from the east. Always the perfect hostess, she provided her guests with the best. If she was reckless, she was also generous. And she had her principles.

George Gordon Moore, with whom Marion frequently played polo, had a luxurious ranch in Carmel Valley, complete with polo field and stables. He lost his fortune and was forced to sell off everything for about a dime on the dollar. Except for the polo ponies. At the auction, prospective buyers were looking forward to a virtual steal of the fine string of horses. Marion was not about to let good horses go for less than their worth, even if she could have had them for a bargain. She attended the auction and, in spite of her own financial difficulties, bid their real value.

Marion had a wide group of friends who had not been ruined by the depression, and there were ways to protect her investment in Pasatiempo. In spite of the cash shortage she had placed herself into, she would almost certainly have weathered her financial crisis had it not been for an automobile accident.

On December 2, 1937, one day before her 45th birthday, Marion was driving back to Pasatiempo when her convertible was struck by a drunken driver. She was put to bed at her home with a severe concussion. The house, as usual, was filled with houseguests, one of whom wrote in the scrapbook:

> This is the cause—sad as it may seem
> That the dynamic Pasatiempo queen
> was absent when all of the matches occurred
> And her house guest qualified second and third.
> But lo! evening fades and sadly, in vain,
> We toast to our hostess in pints of champagne.
> So—happy but wistful, we go to our rest
> Hoping from now on you'll wake with a zest,
> And riding life's waves you'll reach only crest!!!
>
> love, Gertie

She declined medical treatment, but it was almost a half-year before she was again on her feet, and went east for a month. That didn't stop the house party in her Pasatiempo home, however. Another entry in her scrapbook reads:

> May, 1938—on visiting here in Marion's absence...
>
> Oh, you great old ('old' affectionately) Marion
> With your riding coat so tan—
> 'Way off in the East so far
> On account of an accident, to your car...
> You must be quite *the* ornament
> To those out here at Pasatiempo—
> Certainly, it wasn't meant
> Without you, Marion
>
> —Arthur W. Little, Jr.

Marion never really recovered from the accident. Without her, there was no one to promote residential sales, and the financial crisis worsened. In some way the head injuries reorganized her mind. Her personality changed. She became paranoid and secretive.

Her photo of her automobile wreck. Under it in her scrapbook she has written, "Accident December 2nd. December 3rd my birthday. Put to bed."

On the surface, however, life at Pasatiempo continued normally. The guest book is filled with signatures, photos, pretty inscriptions. In December 1938, Marion wrote a cryptic entry, "FCB deal of stock completed. Good news." Once again, Marion was leaning on Cecil Baker, the man who had loaned her money to purchase Pasatiempo a decade earlier, and whom she had rewarded by persuading him to invest in the Kettleman venture. She needed money to meet expenses. Marion Hollins was broke.

Only superficially was all well. In her guest book: "Thank you Marion dear for another restful, lovely visit. Mary [Pickford]." Another course record, 64, on her utopian creation is neatly entered hole by hole against par, with yardages in Marion's meticulous hand. Photographs of her family taken at Beaufort, South Carolina are pasted in. Kim comes, probably to borrow money. Babe Didrickson, now entered in the book as Zaharias, visits. U.S.G.A.'s longtime mentor, Joseph Dey, married to Marion's cousin Rosalie Knapp, signs in.

Underneath the surface, the structure is collapsing. With a touch of her former humor, Marion has form letters printed to answer creditors:

Gentlemen:

We have received your letter of the ____inst and are somewhat surprised at its tone. Evidently, you do not understand our method of handling accounts.

When we receive invoices on the 30th of the month, we put all of them into a large hat, from which five lucky winners are chosen. But in the event that we have any more of your damn foolishness, your name will not even go into the hat.

Sincerely,

The creditors are not amused, and Marion is forced to sell Pasatiempo. For some months she lives on at her home there, but that too is seized, and on November 4, 1940 she leaves. The local paper reports, under a headline *Hail and Farewell:*

It was with genuine regret yesterday that we bade Miss Marion Hollins good-bye as she prepared to leave the Pasatiempo she loved for a new position at Del Monte.

Miss Hollins, as fine a sportswoman as they make, has taken her share of hard knocks in the last decade and always came up smiling. We know it's a shock to leave the property which she watched grow from the bare hills to one of the beauty spots of Santa Cruz, largely through her efforts.

The loss to the city is a major one. We lose an emissary of good will whose shoes will be hard to fill. It's bon voyage to a grand personality!

Shorn of Pasatiempo, Marion spent her last four years living at Pebble Beach. She tried to combat the automobile injuries to her head, and attempted to maintain an outward appearance that all was well, but changes in her behavior, obvious to her friends and niece, were permanent.

The Marion that so many had known was no more.

Results of her concussion took control. She became paranoid, believing a sheriff was pursuing her. She began to hide away small amounts of money, as well as deeds to real estate she still owned, in safe deposit boxes at different banks. She became secretive and erratic. She would arrive unannounced at her young niece's apartment in San Francisco, sleeping bag in hand. Was she "going home" to the only family nearby? Why did she not go to stay with her close friends in Burlingame?

And then she did go to Burlingame, and her niece got a phone call. "It was Ruth Crocker. 'You must come down. Your aunt Marion needs help and we are worried.' I went down, and there was Ruth, Edith Van Antwerp, and Marion who was walking about the living room, talking to herself about being bankrupt, and hearing telephones ringing in her head. I asked her, 'What are friends for if they can't give you some money to do what is right?' Marion didn't answer and left the room. Her friends insisted that she needed to be sent back to her brother, Harry, in Long Island, and that she shouldn't be left alone. They wanted me to take her back on a train. I felt she was suicidal, and they hired a nurse to escort her home. Apparently, she did try to kill herself on the way back.

"She stayed east only for about a month, and then she was back in California."

Wishing You a Jolly Christmas
and a
New Year filled with Happiness

Marion Hollins

Marion Hollins's Christmas card from Pasatiempo, 1930.

Chapter Seventeen

Penultimate Years

*J*n 1941 Marion Hollins was living in Pebble Beach, house-sitting in an arrangement made for her by Samuel Morse, who never ceased to admire her. "A good Joe," he would say about her. Marion had forced herself to accept the tragic loss of Pasatiempo, and although her head injuries from the automobile accident had permanently affected both her mental and physical state, she was again selling real estate and playing golf.

She had qualified for the 1940 Women's National Championship the prior year, but had been defeated in the first round. Now she was practicing for the 1941 Pebble Beach championship.

Marion was still having house parties of one sort or another, "mad balls" in the words of one participant, and her house was filled with golfing friends. One guest, Babe Didrickson, entertained the throng by doing stunts—picking up golf balls with her toes, taking a plate off the table into a full, slow-motion discus throw, vaulting over sofas and chairs in her Olympic hurdle style.

Up early over breakfast, Marion and Didrickson talked golf, and demonstrated swings and putts inside the house. The commotion would awaken the other houseguests, who would stagger down to see what was happening. Golfers remained in stocking feet so that they could speedily hop into their cleats and walk out onto the course. Most guests ate their breakfast in overcoats, as Marion would never turn up the heat anywhere she lived.

Accompanying Marion in her practice rounds, Didrickson was still mastering her game. Before each critical shot she would smile and, using her middle name, say out loud to herself, "Now bear down, Ella."

During the 1941 Pebble Beach championship, in spite of the household of partying friends, Marion paid attention to her own training, and went early to bed. When she lost the tournament she was then back to her old late night tricks. With guests packed into her car, she'd speed down to a Carmel pub for a few late-night drinks. On the return she would invariably tell her nervous passengers, "If I hit that post, I've had too much." She then would accelerate down the hill, approaching the entrance to 17-Mile Drive with its hard right-hand turn and the protecting post. Often she came close.

In 1942, Marion Hollins once again qualified for the Pebble Beach championship. She won it one last time, establishing a record of being an eight-time winner of the trophy.

In the autumn of that year she played an exhibition match against the reigning U.S. Women's Amateur Champion, Betty Hicks.

"I was 21 and Marion was 49," Hicks recalled, "and since I believed physical deterioration was complete by 40, I felt certain I would have no trouble disposing handily of this ebullient mass of cashmere and tweed.... When she walked onto the first tee I was amazed at the shapeless size of her, and then I was even more astonished when she gathered together that mountain of wool and swept into a potent, rhythmic swing...."

Marion won the match, her last match of which there is a record. From then until her death two years later, we know little of her life except for the behavioral changes brought on by her automobile accident.

A few years prior, Grantland Rice, editor of *The American Golfer*, had had Marion pose for a portrait. It appeared as a full-page photograph under the heading "Star of Many Realms." In the picture she sits on a lawn, one arm around an elderly dog, the other couching a white hat with a colored band. She is looking at the camera with an enigmatic smile. The page has the tone of a requiem for the tragedy about to happen. The copy beneath the photo reads, in part: "Miss Marion Hollins of Long Island and California, is something more than a lady golfer good enough to win the National Championship. She has also been one of the star horsewomen of her time, one of the best women polo players in the world, and one of the greatest golf course developers on either the male or the female side.... She is just as able on the business side as she is on the sporting side, with a combination of brains, courage, character and charm...." The text also highlights her creation of the Women's National Golf and Tennis Club, the links at Cypress Point, and Pasatiempo, calling her "the moving spirit and leading star in each of these enterprises."

It is a testimonial to what was.

Chapter Eighteen

The End

*I*n early August of 1944, Marion Hollins' health took a serious turn for the worse. She had been sliding toward this moment for some time. The great spirit which had carried her for over 50 years had siphoned itself off into the atmosphere.

She was 52 years old, and for almost all that time her presence had affected everyone who came into her orbit. When she entered a room of people, something happened, the tenor shifted. Marion Hollins was a large woman with a deep throaty voice, but it wasn't that. It was her tremendous enjoyment and exuberance in the experience of living that poured into all intercourse. Thus the room, and the people in it, changed.

In her crusade as a Suffragette she had carried the bannered motto, "Failure is Impossible." But that had been her motto since earliest childhood. Long before the 21st Amendment gained women the right to vote, she had understood that *possibility,* not impossibility, was what life offered.

Now that ebullient force, which had thrived in the rapture of life's experience, had ebbed. A serious automobile accident, in which she sustained a bad concussion, had cracked the reservoir. News of betrayal by men she had thought she could trust with their stewardship of the Women's National Golf and Tennis Club enlarged the crack. The loss of Pasatiempo drained her will. For a time new springs renewed the spirit, but Marion Hollins was surrendering not to any outside force, but finally to herself.

She was moved from her home at Pebble Beach to a nursing home a few miles away in Pacific Grove. For the first time in her life, a doctor tended to her, but it was too late.

For three weeks she lay there dying. It was in the middle of World War II, and many of her male friends were away. Family was not nearby, and in any case most of them had never held her especially close.

In addition to the surrender, years of hard use and ill care of her body were finally closing down the system. Then on August 28th, the blood vessels in her esophagus ruptured, and in one of the most frightening ways to experience final moments, Marion Hollins drowned in her own blood.

On the death certificate, the doctor listed secondary causes (with question marks after each): *"cirrhosis of liver?, nutritional deficiency?, uterine tumor, carc.?";* and, gleaned from the weeks of caring for his patient, he added *"involutional melancholia."*

Involutional melancholia. Melodious words to express such a signally sad route to death.

Living just a few doors away, a colleague of many years, Henry Puget, head professional at Cypress Point, went about his business ignorant of her condition or proximity. Old friends who would have been there also did not know that she was failing. No family was there, either. Marion Hollins died alone.

Chapter Nineteen

Epilogue

*Marion Hollins after winning the United States Women's
Amateur Championship in 1921.*

In the parlance of tribal or military cultures Marion Hollins would have been called a warrior. She marched into the unknown, armed with ideas and dreams, her weapons to conquer territories ready to be developed. She was never deterred from what she defined as her mission. At the relatively young age of 52 she died.

There is a Japanese folk tale about a peasant who, while hoeing his field, comes across a shell. He brings it home, polishes it, and out of the shell comes a beautiful female genie. Her name is White Wave, and she asks the farmer for his wish. He would like a little more rice, he tells her. From then on he and his family always find a supply of rice at their house. He builds a small temple and places the shell in it. In time, he dies as do the rest of the family, and eventually the little temple collapses. The story concludes: "At the end, all that was left was the story. But that is the way it will be with all of us: all that will be left is the story."

If this book helps perpetuate Marion Hollins's story, it has served the purpose. And if it inspires a renewed interest in her, so much the better. Hollins House, the old clubhouse at Pasatiempo, is named in her memory. Both it and the new clubhouse contain photographs of Marion Hollins and Pasatiempo in her day. There are annual Hollins Trophy tournaments at both Cypress Point Club and Pasatiempo, as well as one sponsored by the Women's Long Island Golf Association. Otherwise, with the exception of a few pockets of knowledge like the wonderful librarians at the Miller Golf Library in Industry City, south of Los Angeles, Marion Hollins is forgotten.

Some of the information I have gathered came from family members as it passed down through the generations of Hollins descendants. After Marion's death, the younger generation would be told that she was "the black sheep" of the family, despite the fact she was the *only* one of her siblings to achieve great things, and is today the only one who is remembered, and monumentalized, as it were, by two sporting venues of incomparable beauty.

More frequent than stories about Marion were amusing stories about Marion's reprobate brothers, who (except for Harry Hollins, Jr. who had a career and large family) were smiled on indulgently and forgiven their "weaknesses" because they had "charm." A grandniece speculates further on this, commenting that, "It was not only that *women* were not valued; neither was *achievement.*"

I began this book by stating that her physical legacies, Cypress Point Club, Pasatiempo, and the now much altered and renamed Women's National Golf and Tennis Club, were insufficient reasons for recalling her life. They do, however, provide a footstep into her life, and are a part of her signature. As she was so much more, however, I prefer to conclude this accounting with what some of those who knew her have said:

> *If there is a keener sportswoman than Miss Marion Hollins of Santa Cruz, in this or any other state, you name her.... In golf she still retains one of the requisites which even champion Glenna Collett loses at times—she is absolutely nerveless.... Topping all these excellences, Miss Hollins is a sport of sports, using the word in its most complimentary sense as all who have ever had any acquaintance with her can vouch.*

—Ventana Free Press, 1931

> *I miss Marion dreadfully. It seems even more so as the months go by. She had so much to give us all of vitality, good cheer, courage, fun and loyalty that it is sad we had to lose her. She can never be replaced.*

—Mary Pickford

I've never known a better sport than Marion Hollins, for money or marbles or fame. In my book of memories, she is at the top of the list marked Thoroughbreds.

—Mildred Yorba MacArthur, in the *National Golfer*, 1959

Marion had a man's mind. She was a visionary, but there was also always a very, very feminine side to her that was appealing, even though she wore severe suits. She was a fantastic dancer. You felt she really enjoyed men, and she always had a lot around.

She had an aura about her. Once, when I was travelling with her on a train this man down the aisle stopped me and said, 'Could you tell me who that person is? Is she famous?' I replied that she was, and he said, 'I was sure of it.' This aura, it wasn't just largeness, it was a force. She took up the room. You had to be strong to be with Marion.

—Phyllis Grissim, her niece

She was one of the outstanding sports women of the world; had been National Golf Champion; was the only good woman polo player I have ever known; was a famous cross-country rider; bought and schooled jumpers for the market; played excellent tennis; and into the bargain had one of the most remarkable personalities I have ever come in contact with. [The number of] her acquaintances was tremendous and she developed into the best saleswoman I have ever known. Her record over a few years in business was astounding.

—S.F.B. Morse, founder of Pebble Beach

I was Miss Hollins' secretary from 1930 to 1940, and anything pertaining to Pasatiempo is always of

interest to me. I would like to point out one fact, how-
ever, that was omitted in the article and that is the
heavy financial burden that Marion Hollins carried
during the depression years as it was no small item to
meet a payroll of over 35 people twice a month when the
outgo was much greater than the income.... She was a
true sport, not only in golf but in her attitude toward life
and the people with whom she dealt. I feel glad that I
knew her and was able to work with someone of her
caliber as I never again met anyone as interesting and
stimulating to work with. Pasatiempo is a fitting memo-
rial to her.

—Frieda C. Zwimpfer, in a letter to
the editor of the *Sentinel*

Miss Hollins was ever-smiling, even-tempered and
loved a good time. She was as friendly with the club
handyman as a high society visitor.... Physically she
was plain looking and stockily built. She would wear the
same skirt and sweater for several days, mainly because
of her easy-going manner and the low priority she put
on outward appearances. 'Her beauty,' said one friend,
'was on an inner quality.'
She was a soft touch for the down-and-out and that,
plus the Depression and some bad investments, de-
pleted her fortune. It was common for her, for example,
to spend $15,000 for a race horse only a step away from
the glue factory.

—Dan Hruby, *San Jose Mercury
News*

To Marion Hollins, the creative genius who built
three country clubs. The 16th hole at Cypress Point
Club—a hole she personally designed—may well be
golf's most beautiful.

To Marion Hollins, the pragmatic dreamer who orchestrated the sprawling Playground of the West— Pasatiempo Country Club and Estates.

To Marion Hollins, financier and feminist, oil wild-catter, social arbiter of the West, beloved friend of the wealthy and celebrated, party giver sans pareil. The slopes of Pasatiempo still echo her laughter.

To Marion Hollins, horsewoman, national golf champion, expert polo player, race car driver, tennis player—perhaps the finest all-around athlete of the 1920s.

—Betty Hicks, former National
Amateur Golf Champion, in a toast
to her memory

It is my opinion that there is no woman in this country who could defeat Miss Hollins if she could be satisfied with playing a woman's game. [However] if she ever played safe in her life I was not there to see it and I have never heard of anyone who was.

—Ann Trabue, reporting on the 1932
Pebble Beach Tournament

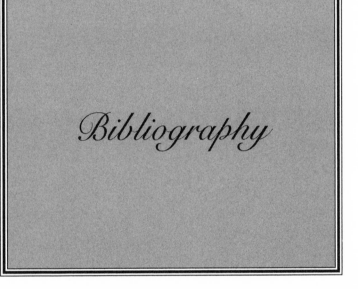

Bibliography

The principal periodicals I relied on were: *American Golfer, Bit and Spur, Country Life, Game and Gossip, Golf Illustrated, National Golfer, New York Herald, New York Herald Tribune, New York Times, New York Tribune, Polo, Pacific Coast Golfer & Poloist, Rider & Driver, The Spur, Town & Country.*

Books

The Last Resorts, Cleveland Amory, Harper & Brothers, New York, 1952.

Who Killed Society? Cleveland Amory, Harper & Brothers, New York, 1960.

The Vanderbilt Era, Louis Auchincloss, Charles Scribner's Sons, New York, 1989.

The Green Book of Golf, 1923–4, Henry Roberts "Bobs," San Francisco, 1924.

The Power Broker, Robert A. Caro, Alfred A. Knopf, New York, 1974.

The Unplayable Lie, Marcia Chambers, Golf Digest/Pocket Books, 1955.

Monterey Place Names, Donald Thomas Clark, Kestrel Press, Carmel Valley, California, 1991.

Ladies in the Rough, Glenna Collett, Alfred A. Knopf, New York, 1929.

Monterey County, the Dramatic Story of its Past, Augusta Fink, Western Tanager Press, Santa Cruz, California, 1972.

In the Rough Land to the South, Susan E. Georgette, University of California, Santa Cruz, 1981.

The Illustrated History of Women's Golf, Rhonda Glen, Taylor Publishing, Dallas, Texas, 1991.

The Aunts, Isabella Halsted, The Sharksmouth Press, 1992.

Along the Great South Bay, Harry W. Havemeyer, Amereon House, Mattituck, New York, 1996.

After the Ball, Eleanor E. Helme, Hurst & Blackett Ltd., London, circa 1931.

The History of Civilization, Elizabeth Coles Morris Hollins, privately printed, 1930.

The Pasatiempo Story, Margaret Koch, Pasatiempo Golf Club, Santa Cruz, California, 1990.

Swinging into Golf, Ernest Jones, Whittlesey House, New York, 1937.

The Old Oakdale History, Elizabeth Kuss, William K. Vanderbilt Historical Society, Oakdale Long Island, 1983.

The History of the Cypress Point Club, Roger D. Lapham, Jr., Cypress Point Club, 1997.

Golf, Cecil Leitch, Thornton Butterworth Ltd., London, 1922.

Scotland's Gift, Golf, Charles Blair Macdonald, Charles Scribner's Sons, New York, 1928.

Golf Architecture, Alister MacKenzie, Classics of Golf Stamford, Connecticut, reprint edition of the 1920 edition.

The Spirit of St. Andrews, Alister MacKenzie, Sleeping Bear Press, Chelsea, Michigan, 1995.

Fifty Years of American Golf, H.B. Martin, Dodd, Mead & Company, New York, 1936.

The World Is So Full, Dorothy McBurney Noyes, privately printed, Islip Long Island, 1953.

Untold Friendships, Schuyler Livingston Parsons, Houghton Mifflin Company, Boston, 1955.

The Jones Golf Swing and Other Suggestions, John Godfrey Saxe, privately printed, 1949.

California and Other States of Grace, Phyllis Theroux, William Morrow and Company, New York, 1980.

A Gallery of Women Golfers, Enid Wilson, Country Life Limited, London, 1961.

*Marion Hollins at her doorway, near the end of
her days at Pasatiempo.*

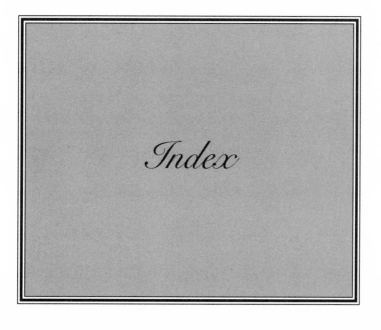

Index